ABANDONED *but* NOT ALONE

A True Story about the Pain of Abandonment and How to Find Hope, Healing, and Happiness

GRACE REACHER

ISBN 979-8-88616-082-6 (paperback)
ISBN 979-8-88616-083-3 (digital)

Christian Faith Publishing
832 Park Avenue
Meadville, PA 16335
www.christianfaithpublishing.com

Printed in the United States of America

DEDICATION

I want to dedicate this book to my beloved husband, soulmate, mentor, and best friend of almost 25 years. His love, support, and encouragement have nudged me gently over the years to get outside of my comfort zone, believe in myself, and soar to new heights to reach the potential he saw in me all along. Thanks for believing in me, babe. What a blessed season we had together until God took you home for eternity. I'm grateful that you are healed and at peace with our Heavenly Father.

I also want to honor my daughter, who has always been a friend and a joy to me. She has gone through everything with me and knows me better than anyone. She has always been a great sounding-board who shares ideas and thoughts to give me a better perspective. Thank you for all you have done to encourage me as I stepped towards my dream of becoming an author.

Thanks to my mom, who dedicated her life to my wellbeing. Thank you for all the things you did for me that I never knew. As a child, I couldn't see what you were going through. As a parent and grandparent, I can see more clearly. Thank you for loving me through all the challenges I put you through. I love you mom.

I also want to thank my friend and author Joyce Norman for always encouraging me to follow my dreams and write what is on my heart. If it weren't for you continuously encouraging me over the years to write, this book would never have happened.

I am with you always.

—Matthew 28:20

INTRODUCTION

In this story, you will read a true story about love, loss, lessons, and true love found. You will discover the answer how to be victorious over all of life's challenges. I chose to write this in third person because I believe it made the story easier to tell. Names were changed to protect the privacy of the characters.

In the lessons learned, there are a lot of pain and tears along the way as a young child learns about loss early in life. Discover how believing the lie of abandonment shaped Gracie's life and affected all of her relationships and decisions. This story is not sad but one of victory over battle scars—a journey in life of fighting our own personal demons and winning.

Scars are a good thing; they remind us of where we have been and what we have overcome. Abandonment is a lie from the enemy that we must choose not to believe and adopt as our thought process. Don't pitch a tent and live in the lies. Instead, move your tent, and pitch it in the land of hope.

Move your tent. (Genesis 13:18)

I will live in Hope. (Acts 2:26)

So how do we find peace? When we allow
His Spirit to control our minds, we are filled with
life and peace. (Romans 8:6)

My husband always said the worst part about divorce is that the kids become innocent victims in the battle. That is true; fortunately, there can still be hope. Our story doesn't have to end in tragedy.

Adonai's, our God, eternal purposes are being worked out through our difficulties. Our troubles are part of His majestic master plan, and they are achieving an eternal glory that far outweighs them all! Every valley has a purpose. Don't waste the pain.

His grace is sufficient for me. I glory in my weaknesses because, in my weaknesses, He is made strong (2 Corinthians 12:9). Stand on our Father's Word. When the enemy lies to you and labels you with a negative spirit that torments you, recognize and rebuke it. When you know Adonai's Word, you can speak His Word to the enemy when he tries to stick his untruths on you. To know the Father's Word, we must study it every day.

As my dear friend always says, "We can choose to sit in the mud or dance in the rain." That statement is so true; each of us has a choice. In the beginning, a child is dependent on Adonai to carry them through until they are old enough to make their own decisions. When you reach the age of maturity (for me, it was fourteen), that's when you "choose this day who you will serve" (Joshua 24:15).

Whether your battle is with abandonment or a list of other evil spirits, this story will inspire you not to give up. Find hope, discover your purpose, and find your identity in truth, in your heavenly Father. When you make the choice to allow our heavenly Father to have your heart, He holds your hand and directs your path. Cling to Him.

> Adonai directs a person's steps, and He delights in their way. We may stumble, but we won't fall headlong, for He holds us by the hand. (Psalm 37:23–24)

What wonderful news to know that if we stray off of His path, He is with us, directing us gently back on course. It may be quite bumpy off-road, but He gets us back on path, if we are willing to allow Him to help.

Let us rejoice that even though Satan attacks with lies and murderous intent, the Holy Spirit (Ruach Hakodesh) can render our enemies harmless. We will fulfill our purposes in Adonai if we cling to Him! When you feel alone, know His Word, take comfort in His promises.

His Word says in John 16:32, "I am not alone; the Father is with me," and Matthew 27:20, "I am always with you." These promises got me through every battle.

Another passage that I often repeat, pray this to get you through the toughest of storms:

> But now thus says Adonai, He who created you, O Jacob, He who formed you, O Israel:
> "Fear not, for I have redeemed you;
> I have called you by name; you are mine.
> When you pass through the waters,
> I will be with you;
> and through the rivers, they shall not overwhelm you;
> when you walk through the fire, you shall not be burned,
> and the flame shall not consume you.
> For I am Adonai your God, the Holy One of Israel, your Savior.
> I give Egypt as your ransom, Cush and Seba, in exchange for you.
> Because you are precious in My eyes and honored, and I love you, I give men in return for you, peoples, in exchange for your life." (Isaiah 43:1–3)

That passage always reminds me how much my heavenly Father loves me and is with me every minute of every day. I do *not* walk alone! No matter what comes my way, He is with me. I cling to my hope in Him.

When it seems that He isn't speaking to you and all is quiet when you pray, remember this: the teacher is always silent during the test. You are not left behind; you are not set aside. You are *set apart* by your heavenly Father for a special purpose. You can only discover this purpose through seeking more of Him in His Word. You are chosen and set apart for Him (Zephaniah 1:7; John 17:17, 19).

Don't allow anyone to tell you that you are not special. Find true Shalom peace and purpose in His Word. I find reading the whole story, the whole Bible, brings me the hope and peace I've always been searching. His peace transcends all understanding (Philippians 4:6–7).

I spent a lifetime searching for a love that only my heavenly Father could give me. Once I discovered that truth, my whole life changed. I could finally see clearly; I could see things through His eyes. He loves us so much (Romans 5:8, 1 John 4:18–19).

In addition to reading the whole Bible from Genesis to Revelations, pray. Prayer is not a skill set; it's a mindset (Isaiah 55). If you are not sure how to pray, you will find a prayer guide at the back of the book. I pray that you find your hope and peace in Adonai today and through reading my story.

> May Adonai bless you and keep you.
> May Adonai make his face shine upon you
> and show you his favor.
> May Adonai lift up his face toward you and
> give you peace. (Numbers 6:24–26)

CHAPTER 1

Reminiscing

It was a beautiful, hot, humid late Fall day in the South that still felt like the heat of the summer, the kind of day that you could only enjoy from looking through the window from an air-conditioned room. Bees were buzzing. Mosquitos were whizzing by looking for someone to bite. There was the ever-present swarm of gnats that hovered over the yard, circling in a frenzy, seeming to be in a hurry but going nowhere. Birds were chirping flying from feeder to feeder while the squirrels bounced around looking for something to eat. Just normal routines in the backyard; Wally always loved to sit on the patio with a glass of wine and just watch the activity in the afternoons as the sun was getting ready to call it a day. Today there was a different viewpoint.

Earlier Gracie, who was tiny five feet nothing, had climbed up in the hospital bed with her sweet husband, Wally, who used to be 6'3", 225, and a very muscular bodybuilder. For weeks now, his hospital bed had been positioned in the den in front of the plate glass window so that he could still view his beloved backyard and the nature activity. She had spent the first part of the day doing her routine as of late, getting the house in order for the day, helping the sitter with caring for Wally. Gracie was grateful for every moment that God gave them together. It didn't matter to them that it was the year of the COVID and the whole world was shut down for the first time in history. In her opinion, it worked in their favor that she was shut in with him and able to keep him home and have access to an amazing hospice team that came to them. She felt so blessed that his mind was sharp till the end so that they could still have conversations and reminisce together. They laughed, and they cried while they enjoyed snuggling and recounting their lives together. Both of them marveled at how much they had each changed and grown during their time together. Where did the time go? They could vividly remember their dating days over twenty-three years ago. Now their time together was coming to an end; there was still so much they wanted to do together. Since they couldn't do more, they chose to focus on all the memories they had together, including the blessing of being able to talk about not only their past but plan for Gracie's future without him. They snuggled and reminisced every night during those last weeks.

After getting him settled that particular day, Gracie lay snugged up next to him again, holding his hand, with her chin resting on his shoulder as she gazed out the window while he talked. As he was telling a story she had heard before, her mind wandered as she stared out the window. Absentmindedly, Gracie wondered what the purpose was for the swarming gnats that never seem to do anything but swarm in a circle. Her mind continued to drift as he talked, and she thought back over their life and how quickly they got to this point. How blessed they felt to have each other. They often shared their wonder at how much God must love them to have put them together. Mere weeks away from their nineteenth wedding anniversary; and Gracie caught herself wondering if he would make it till then.

As she listened to him talk, she thought back over their life together and how happy they had been. To them, it was like a fairy tale love that people only dreamt of having, and they lived it. The years together flew by while they raised her two children from a previous marriage. Their youngest daughter Caroline had recently married. Then Wally retired from his consultant job, and they were ready to enjoy retirement when suddenly all their plans changed with one unexpected health diagnosis. She thought of who she was when they met—insecure, lacking any self-esteem or self-confidence—and how his love for her had changed her. She always believed that God had sent him to her as a special gift, in the most unique way, and God used him to help her heal and open her heart again. God and Wally had totally changed her life throughout their years together.

Lying there together snuggling, her thoughts were interrupted when she heard the rhythm of his voice inflection change and his hand tighten around hers. She leaned back and looked up at him when she noticed tears streaming down his face. He had begun reciting the twenty-third Psalm to her. Gracie smiled with pride through her own wet eyes as he spoke it to her without missing a word. He surprised himself at his memory and laughed through tears as Gracie gasped and grinned at him with surprise and pride. Wally shared the story of how his mom made him go to church every Sunday as a kid and how his Sunday school teacher was relentless making sure he memorized the Psalm. He couldn't believe he still remembered verbatim. Gracie didn't think she could love him more until that moment; her heart almost exploded with renewed love for him. He was her world; she adored him and couldn't imagine what life would be for her without him. As he continued to chatter anxiously, Gracie was praying under her breath, trying to muster all the strength that God would give her to hold it together. It was hard for both of them to believe that their time together was coming to an end. How did they get here? They hadn't had enough time.

He interrupted her thoughts again as she heard him tell her he wasn't afraid to die; he just wasn't ready to leave her. With a look of desperate concern on his face, he nervously asked Gracie, "Who is going to take care of you? Who will you talk to when you have situations you need help with? I don't want to leave you. I feel like I'm abandoning you." It was his last comment that made her breath catch in her throat and triggered her emotions. Gracie's heart had been severely scarred from early childhood, and she had spent a lifetime fighting the fear of abandonment.

Her early fears had affected every relationship in her life. Everyone that came into her life she feared that they would leave her. It didn't cause her to withdraw and not let people in; on the contrary, she was always hopeful and wanted people in her life. Her personality was one to love you right away until you gave her a reason not to love you. Even then, when people left her life, she never stopped caring about them; it was her nature to love others, regardless of how much pain they might cause her. So it was very difficult for her to make friends because she would try too hard to be liked. As a result, people would feel smothered and not want to be a part of her life. It would crush her, or she would destroy the friendship before they could leave her. She was always desperate to be liked and wanted and could never find anyone that wanted her in their life long-term. As a child growing up, she tried to be the best friend, the best daughter, the best sister, the best grandchild; but she seemed to always feel left out, set aside, never chosen, never wanted.

It was then when Wally was sharing his heart and telling her how concerned he was and how he didn't want to "abandon" her that she had a sudden revelation. Tears began to stream down Gracie's face as the thought occurred to Gracie that he might be "abandoning" her, but he was not leaving her alone. The Gracie he was leaving behind was not the Gracie he had married so many years ago; she was going to be okay.

Through their years together, Adonai had healed her heart and her scars mostly transparent now. Her fear of abandonment no longer had a hold on her; Adonai had transformed her and changed her life. As the revelation grew, her mind took her back to where her journey began when she was first abandoned, and her innocent childhood world fell apart.

CHAPTER 2

Innocence Stolen

It was a gloomy fall afternoon. The birds chirped in the trees above, and the golden leaves had been falling and blanketed the ground, making it look like a golden carpet of leaves. Gracie and her best friend and cousin Jules sat on the swings in the backyard at Jules's house, talking like two best friend cousins always had. Today was different though. Gracie, whose nickname had always been Giggles, was not her happy giggling self. She was so sad, lost in thought, as she slowly moved back and forth in the swing, kicking the golden leaves that had fallen to the ground. Jules didn't notice at first. She was chattering away about something which was normal for her. She always got so excited when Gracie came over and couldn't wait to tell her the latest stories she knew about anything and nothing just to talk. Jules said something that she expected Gracie to laugh about and realized Gracie wasn't paying attention. That's when she knew something was wrong but wasn't sure what. She waited for Gracie to say something; after a long silence, she finally asked her what was wrong. With tears in her eyes, she looked over at Jules and said, "I hate being seven years old; this is the worst year of my life." Gracie had just found out that her mom and dad were getting divorced.

In her young life, she had so many fond memories of her dad. She thought he hung the moon. He wasn't a perfect dad, but to her, he could do no wrong. Her dad was extremely handsome, 6'2", 195 lbs., dark hair, green eyes, always tanned, and was a great dancer. He had a great sense of humor and what women viewed as amazing sex appeal. From her view, she thought he was beautiful, fun, and the perfect father. She remembered him as almost always having an alcoholic drink in one hand with a cigarette between his first two fingers of the same hand. When she watched TV back then, she thought that he could pass as Dean Martin's twin. Was he trying to be like him? She would never know, but they sure looked like brothers with looks and mannerisms.

Gracie loved it when her dad would take her for rides on the back of his motorcycle. She cherished the moments when they watched their favorite TV shows together while she sat in his lap, and they ate junk food together. Her favorite movies were the scary ones with Vincent Price because it was fun to snuggle in his shoulder and let him protect her. She could hardly wait for him to get home from work each day; sadly, there were so many days that he didn't come home until late, and she was already in bed. On the days when she and her brother would get in trouble, their mom would always say, "Wait until your dad gets home." Looking back, Gracie wondered if he avoided coming home most nights until after they were in bed so he wouldn't have to deal with discipline. He wanted to be the fun dad. As soon as he got home, he would get the story and then be expected to head up the stairs. He would talk to Gracie's brother first and then spank him. Gracie always waited, silently praying and crying as she waited in anticipation of her turn. When he got to Gracie's room, she would immediately cry as he opened the door; he would melt every time. Then he would hug her and tell her to do better. She wasn't manipulating him; she had spent all afternoon beating herself up and planned never to do it again. When he walked through the door, she would start crying and promising never to do it again. She meant it, and he believed it.

One of her favorite memories was when he came home from work one day, and she was in her room awaiting his discipline for her latest childhood bright idea. You see, her idea came from a recent visit to Grannie's home. She loved going to Grannie's because she always had something fun going on. Gracie thought she was such a fun grandmother. She was a sweet, sophisticated five-foot woman who worked for the government but loved to spend time with her grandkids. She didn't learn how to drive until she was a widow her second time in her early sixties. Grannie was a little eccentric, artistic, and had a creative imagination. At this particular time, Gracie was about four years old. When they went for their weekly visit, Gracie walked into Grannie's home and gasped with sheer delight. What she saw was the most beautiful artwork she had ever seen. Grannie had drawn a mural of purple irises on an entire wall with pastels. All she wanted to do that day was stare at the picture, taking in every detail of the flowers. For days after this visit, all Gracie could think about was this beautiful mural. She then came up with what she thought was a great plan. While her mom was busy one day and told Mark and Gracie to play until dinnertime, Gracie decided this was the perfect time to implement her plan. Without telling her brother, she grabbed her crayons and set out to draw a mural just like Grannie's on the wall in the hall between hers and Mark's bedrooms. She was so excited to recreate this masterpiece and surprise everyone.

Much to her disappointment, Gracie quickly realized that flowers were harder to draw than she thought, so she devised a new plan. Quickly she came up with a plan B for her mural to use different color crayons and make lots of beautiful circles. Gracie felt confident that she could master making pretty colorful circles that everyone would love. Before she could complete her masterpiece though, Mark came up and interrupted her flow; he caught her in the act. He went running down the stairs, screaming for Mom to come to see what Gracie had done.

Gracie could not understand why her mom was so upset. She was trying to express her artistic talents just as Grannie had done. Gracie thought it turned out very pretty, if only her mom would have allowed her to finish. Having had time to think about what she had done while waiting on her dad to get home, she reasoned in her mind that her dad would undoubtedly understand. To her delight, he was very amused by her desire and reasoning to create this masterpiece for their home. He then invited Gracie to help him repaint the wall with regular house paint to match the rest of the house. He told her that since her mom didn't like murals at their home, he bet Grannie would let her help next time she painted a mural. Gracie's hero came up with what she thought was a great idea. She told him he was the best dad in the world; she adored him. These were some of the memorable moments he spent with her; there weren't many, but she clung to them.

Her parents worked a lot and went on business trips often. She and her brother had a great nanny, but Gracie wanted to be with her parents. They used to host these home parties with their best friends who brought their kids. It was okay playing with the kids, but Gracie rather have danced with the adults. Her mom played the piano, and it was so fun to watch. She was mesmerized by her mom's talent at playing, and her songs were so fun for dancing. It was no wonder Gracie wanted to hang out with them instead of the other kids. Her favorite times were when her dad would call to her where she was sitting on the steps, watching and inviting her to dance with him. It was the fun, fast dances, not the slow ones. She just giggled and giggled, enjoying every minute.

Gracie had no idea that her parents were having problems, so it came as quite a surprise when her mom told her they were getting a divorce. She was devastated. So many thoughts were racing through her head while she was sharing the story with Jules. She said, "How could he leave me? Doesn't he love me anymore? Was it something I did? Was it my fault? What did I do?" Jules had no idea what to say; she just listened as Gracie shared and cried.

Gracie was so tenderhearted that it made it even harder for her to adjust to the reality of her dad leaving, making it impossible for her to hide her pain. In Gracie's mind, she had been abandoned by her dad, it was her fault, and there was nothing that anyone could say to make her feel differently. Unknowingly, this thought process would take root and affect all her relationships for many many years to come. Her mom tried everything she could think of to cheer her up. Knowing how much Gracie loved to dance at their home parties, she decided to put Gracie in dance classes hoping that would help cheer her. Gracie did love the costumes and dancing around, but the long practices seemed to cause her physical pain.

At that time, most likely her mom wasn't thinking about the complications surrounding Gracie's birth. While her mom was pregnant with Gracie, she contracted the mumps. She was very sick, and the doctor was concerned about the side effects of the sickness and how it might affect Gracie's health. The doctor told her that it would be a miracle if she were able to walk. After her birth, they discovered complications with her hips. The doctor worked to correct the issues with her hips by using braces for a time. She had to wear the braces at night when she went to sleep. Her brother Mark couldn't bear to hear her cry and would sneak in there sometimes and unscrew the bar; she would stop crying right away. When Gracie began walking, she had difficulty walking with her feet straight. Still, with therapy and constant reminding from her mom to focus on walking with toes forward, she was able to overcome the challenge. They were grateful for the miracle but quickly moved on with life. Not knowing there were underlying problems, they had no way of knowing that the problems would arise later and that the pain would suddenly show up with strenuous exercise. It was years before they tied the scenarios together.

So while Gracie was crying, telling her mom that it hurt her hips to dance for so long at a time, it didn't occur to anyone that the problem was related to Gracie's earlier issues with her hips. At that time, her mom had a full plate, and it was easy to think Gracie was just being difficult. She had spent so much money getting her into dance, juggling all the practices with work and getting Mark to his football practices as a single parent. It was frustrating for her mom that Gracie didn't want to stick with it after all her effort. She begged her mom to take her out of dance; she relented.

This incident caused Gracie to feel that she had let her mom down, thus making her sadder than when she started. For Gracie, she lost her dad and now felt like her mom hated her. Her heart suffered a more significant loss from their disagreement. At this point, Gracie felt like a failure and that no one loved her or wanted her.

Gracie's mom had so much pressure on her as a single parent trying to make ends meet with no child support; it was a tough time for all. Her brother, Mark, seemed to internalize his pain. Her brother was five years older than her, so they weren't close and didn't talk about their pain together.

In an effort to find something for Gracie to do to take her mind off of her dad leaving, her mom came up with another idea. Since Gracie loved her mom's piano playing so much, she decided to put her in piano lessons. Gracie was nervous but excited. She imagined what it would be like to play the piano like her mom; this seemed like a good idea to her.

You see, Gracie is a sensitive, tenderhearted girl with a mission to make everyone smile. If she can't make you smile, her way to deal with the disappointment is to withdraw. She has a habit of withdrawing when there is any screaming, fighting, or bullying behavior. Gracie was allowing herself to come out of her withdrawn state and try the piano thing. She had heard girlfriends in school talking about their piano lessons, so she wanted to try it.

While sitting in class on a gloomy, overcast fall day, the teacher was going on and on about something she was teaching, but Gracie wasn't listening. All Gracie could think about was being a piano player like her mom. She was daydreaming of her and her mom playing songs together and how fun that would be. In her mind, Gracie felt this would make her mom happy. She told herself that this would make her mom like her again and surely forgive her for quitting dance lessons.

Gracie looked up at the clock with excitement because there were only a few minutes left in the school day. Surely no one has ever been more excited than she was for the school day to be over. This day would be her first day of piano practice, and her mom was getting off work early to come to pick her up and take her to the lesson.

The bell rang, and Gracie was the first to jump up, ready to go. Finally, the time had come to start a new adventure. It was an exciting day! She had made up her mind that she was going to be the best piano player ever, and it was going to make her mom so happy.

With butterflies in her stomach, Gracie was determined to make this work. What began as a cool, crisp day had turned into a wet, darker, gloomier day. Anticipation growing in her stomach, Gracie stepped out of the car onto the damp, dark brown leaves that were everywhere in the teacher's yard. As she looked down at the leaves, she wondered if they were darker today. Gracie ran around the car and grabbed her mom's hand, and they walked to the front door together.

The week before, they had stopped in for a visit to meet with the teacher; her mom wanted to make sure it was a good fit. Determined to make this work, Gracie chose to look for the positives in the visit. As the teacher and Gracie's mom discussed details, Gracie clung to her mom while looking around to size things up in her mind. What seemed like hair standing up on her neck, Gracie did not feel good about this; the teacher and her home seemed like a scary place. It reminded Gracie of the *Hansel and Gretel* story.

At first glance and while listening to her talk, Gracie determined in her mind that the teacher must be one hundred years old; she seemed ancient from Gracie's eight-year-old, little, three-foot-tall point of view. Wait! Her gaze on the old lady suddenly froze. Was it her imagination, or did she have a hooked nose with a large hairy mole on it? Gracie imagined that she looked like the scary lady in the *Hansel and Gretel* story and was frozen in place staring while she remembered the story details.

Suddenly, Gracie remembered that her mom always said, "It is not nice to stare," so she made a determined effort to look away and focus on something else. As she looked around the home, her mind stayed on the runaway-train thought process. Gracie felt confident that it looked like the scary lady's house in the story.

Lost in her thoughts, wondering how many kids this woman ate that never got to see their mom and dad again, Gracie slowly drifted out of her daydreaming as she heard her mom ask her what she thought about taking lessons there. Despite the foreboding, uneasy feeling she had, she wanted so badly to make her mom happy, so she said yes. Gracie decided to pretend the scary lady with the hooked nose and giant hairy mole was a sweet Grannie like hers and that the home was a fun dollhouse where you get to drink milk and eat all the cookies you want. Wait! Isn't that how she lured Hansel and Gretel into her house?

CHAPTER 3

Piano Lessons

As they stood outside the front door, Gracie's mom rang the doorbell. While they waited for the teacher to answer the door, anxiety got the best of Gracie. So many thoughts were racing through Gracie's mind. Had she made the wrong decision by saying yes? Would this scary lady eat her like Hansel and Gretel? Was her mom trying to get rid of her by leaving her there with the scary lady? Did she imagine it all, and she was a lovely lady? Gracie was trying not to focus on her fears but instead on her mom being proud of her. All of this wouldn't matter once they got to play songs together on the piano. She knew it was too late to turn back now; swallowing a feeling of dread, she mustered up a smile. As the door slowly began to open, Gracie held her breath as she waited to see if the old lady appeared dressed in a witch's outfit.

The teacher opened the door with a kind smile and moved back for Gracie to enter. As Gracie walked through the door, she turned to wait on her mom. Much to her surprise, her mom didn't come in this time. She told her bye and said she would be back to pick her up later. At that moment, such fear arose in her; there was no doubt in Gracie's mind that she had made a huge mistake by saying yes. Gracie thought to herself that this was the last time she would ever see her mom. Tears welled up in her eyes as she realized her mom had just abandoned her and that she would never see her again.

The door shut behind her; that was it, no turning back. Not knowing what to do, she just went through the motions, doing what the scary old lady told her to do. It was challenging to focus on what the teacher said because her fears were racing out of control. When the teacher corrected her mistakes in a harsh tone, Gracie would cringe. Gracie withdraws when someone screams at her; lessons were not going well. Gracie was so nervous and kept making mistakes. The more mistakes she made, the more the teacher reacted, and the more mistakes she made out of nervousness.

The teacher was getting agitated at her for continuing to make mistakes. Gracie tried hard, but her heart wasn't in it. Didn't the teacher realize that she was upset that her mom was never coming back to get her? The teacher suddenly pulled out a ruler and slapped the piano with it to get her attention. It was all she could do not to break down crying. The more she corrected her, the more challenging it was for her to focus. She was trying so hard to be brave.

Suddenly there was a knock at the door; Gracie was so relieved to have a break from the constant correction and ruler slapping on the piano. As she was looking around, making a plan for her escape, Gracie heard her mom's voice. She jumped up and ran to the door. Gracie had never been more excited to see her mom. She ran past the teacher into her mom's arms. The session was over, and Gracie was so relieved that her mom came back to get her. Gracie didn't tell her mom what had happened; she was too relieved that she came back to get her, realizing that she hadn't abandoned her after all.

Every afternoon when they got home, Gracie's mom made her practice the piano for at least thirty minutes. She didn't want to practice; she was too busy developing a plan to get a new piano teacher. How was she to tell her that the teacher was mean and verbally abusing her?

Assuming that all was well, Gracie's mom dropped her off the following week for lessons. Gracie had no idea how she would tell her about this woman without her getting mad at her. She knew her mom would be upset again if she quit. If she had heard it once, she heard it a hundred times, "No one likes a quitter." Gracie didn't want to be a quitter; she just wanted a friendly teacher. She had big plans to play the piano with her mom; how would she fix this? Her friends at school talked about their nice piano teachers, confirming in her mind that they existed. She just needed a plan to convince her mom to move her to another teacher. What if she couldn't develop a plan before the teacher lured her in with the milk and cookies, never to be seen again?

This internal battle went on for several weeks; fortunately, she only went to lessons once a week. Gracie lived a couple of streets over from the teacher, so her mom decided for her to walk from school to practice and then walk home from the teacher's house. They lived close to the school as well.

Over the short time she took lessons, the teacher got more verbally violent with her, constantly slapping the ruler on the piano for emphasis. Gracie never saw any milk and cookies, but on one particular day, the teacher lost control and slapped Gracie's knuckles with the ruler. Gracie gasped and grabbed her hand, holding it close to protect it from another slap. Tears were welling up in her eyes; she just glared at the woman waiting for her to hit her again. Thankfully she regained her composure. Gracie took that as an opportunity to grab her book bag and run home.

As she ran out the door, she never looked back, crying all the way home. She dreaded telling her mother she was quitting, but she couldn't go back. The thought of running away crossed her mind, but she didn't want to run away; she wanted her mom to listen to her side of the story and believe her this time. Sadly, things did not go as she had hoped, and she was labeled a quitter. Her mom told her that she would not spend any more money on activities to quit before finishing. Gracie was so sad that her mom wouldn't let her explain.

Gracie knew that her mom must surely hate her now after quitting piano. Whether it was true or not, that's how Gracie perceived her reaction. She felt so alone at this point. Her dad had abandoned her physically, and now she felt like her mom abandoned her mentally. At this point, Gracie believed that no one loved her or believed in her. Thus, causing her to lose all self-esteem and self-confidence that an eight-year-old should have. Not knowing what her mother was dealing with as a result of being abandoned by her husband—

the love of her life, Gracie misread her mom's actions to mean that she didn't love or want Gracie. Not knowing who to turn to, Gracie focused on trying to stay out of trouble. She bent over backward, trying to be the best kid so that her mom would maybe love her then. Gracie always believed that Mark was Mom's favorite, but he always seemed to be in trouble for something, so Gracie thought that would make it easier to become the favorite if she was super good and didn't cause Mom any trouble. Over time, she realized that plan wasn't going to work either. Her backup plan was to cling to her grannie and her nanny that both adored Gracie. She thought that maybe if she spent more time with them, her mom would appreciate the break from the stresses of caring for her.

Gracie spent many nights over at Nannie Molly's home; she called her aunt Molly. She didn't have a little girl, so she loved dressing Gracie up. Aunt Molly would curl Gracie's hair with sponge rollers and buy her dolls; Gracie loved being at her home. Gracie was the daughter Aunt Molly never had.

Her grannie came up with a great idea to cheer Gracie; she decided to pierce her ears. One weekend, when Gracie stayed with Grannie, her mom walked in right as Grannie rubbed ice on her ear lobe before stabbing it with a regular needle. She loved her grannie and trusted her completely. At the time, Gracie had no idea how bad it would hurt; she just wanted to have pierced ears to go with her curls that Aunt Molly made. Her mom thought Grannie had lost her mind and was not happy about it. After some convincing from both Grannie and Gracie, her mom relented. When the needle went through Gracie's ear, she gasped, screamed, and burst into tears. It was so painful that she wouldn't let her grannie touch the other ear.

Her mom insisted that a professional needed to do it. As badly as it hurt, she still wanted to get her ears pierced. Her mom made an appointment with her pediatrician which, at the time, they would do ear piercings. Gracie was so excited once the doctor pierced her ears. Surely curls and pierced ears would make everything better in her life.

Gracie did become a cheerleader a couple of times through her childhood and completed the season each time, but it wasn't her passion. She was still searching to find her passion. A couple of years later, as she was slowly adjusting to their new life without her dad living with them, it seemed things were turning around. Her parents were working things out and were talking about getting remarried. Gracie was ecstatic when they finally told her. She could hardly wait for her dad to be back home with them again.

They were going to be a family again, and everything was going to be perfect this time.

CHAPTER 4

Here We Go Again!

Things at home seemed like they were going well. Gracie was so excited to have her dad back home. She was hoping to spend more time with him now that he was back. In her mind, if she were a better daughter this time, he would not want to leave her again.

Gracie, much like her mom; always wanted to help people in need. She was bubbly, outgoing, always had a smile, and loved to make others laugh. When Gracie met someone, she had the type of personality where she loved them right away and wanted them to feel loved. That's why it was so difficult for her to understand when someone didn't like her.

When Gracie was in fourth grade, she was the tiniest girl in class and had an innate joyful disposition in spite of troubles at home. Sadly, her size and positive demeanor put her in a position to be bullied. A girl in her class named Mandy seemed to make it her mission to wipe the smile off Gracie's face. She tried so hard to get the girl to like her, but the more Gracie tried, the more she made fun of her. Then one day, Mandy suddenly didn't come to school for a week. When she returned, Gracie knew something was up. Mandy wasn't speaking to anyone and seemed sad about something. Even though she was always mean to Gracie, she had to check on her and find out what was wrong. It wasn't in Gracie's nature to allow someone to hurt in her presence and not help them. She knew she wasn't the girl's problem. She had never done anything to make her hate her. She had to see if she could put a smile back on the girls face.

That night when Gracie's mom picked her up from Aunty Molly's, she explained to her mom what had happened. As it turned out, Mandy's stepdad had died in a car accident recently. Her mom and stepdad had been out to dinner and to a party with friends. He drove the babysitter home; and on his way back, instead of turning left to go up the hill to their home, he turned right off a ravine into a ditch, killing him instantly. She was distraught and said her mom told her that she needed a job now, or they would be homeless. Gracie assured her everything would be okay. She told her that she would pray for her and that she would talk to her mom and see how she can help. As Gracie had hoped, her mom came to the rescue. Her mom owned her own business and wanted to help; she hired Mandy's mom as a secretary for the office.

As was their nature, Gracie and her mom helped them in any way they could. Gracie and Mandy became friends at school and were playing together every day. Mandy was no longer mean to Gracie. When all of this happened, Gracie discovered why Mandy had been mean to her. Mandy told Gracie that her parents fought all the time. She said that Gracie was always happy at school, and it upset her because her home life was not good. And she wanted to be happy like Gracie. That comment sent Gracie on a mission to bring as much joy to Mandy's life as possible. She prayed for Mandy and her family when she said her nightly prayers.

Gracie asked her mom if they could come over for dinner since they didn't have any money. Her mom often invited Mandy and her mom and brother over for dinner to help out until they could get on their feet. Mandy was thrilled, and she and Gracie became fast friends. Everyone was happy and enjoying hanging out together. All of them were inseparable. Most days, they either hung out at Gracie's home or at theirs. Gracie was so happy to have been able to help this family and help bring joy to their lives.

It wasn't too long before Gracie started noticing that things seemed off with her parents. At first, her dad was hanging out with them when Mandy and her family came over. Suddenly her dad was working late a lot again. Then suddenly Mandy's mom stopped accepting dinner invitations, and she was acting strange at school again. She had gone back to making fun of Gracie again and being mean to her. It was very confusing, Gracie wondered, *What was going on?*

One night, Gracie's mom decided she and the kids would take dinner to Mandy's house and visit for a bit. She had called to let Mandy's mom know that they were coming. It had been a while since they had dinner together. Did Gracie's mom suspect something? Was this a test to gather information? Before they could get everything together to leave home to head over to Mandy's house, Gracie's dad called. Gracie and her brother waited on the bed next to their mom until she got off the phone. Gracie was hoping that he would not work late that night, rather come home in time to go with them to Mandy's house or meet them there. Her mom sounded upset, and after hanging up the phone, she sat staring at the floor.

"Mom, what's wrong?" they asked in unison.

The color seemed to have gone out of her face as she said, "We aren't going to take them dinner after all."

Gracie asked, "Why? I want to go see them." She wanted to find out why Mandy was acting mean to her again.

Her mom replied slowly, "Your dad just said that he is having an affair with Mandy's mom. He says he loves her and isn't coming back home." She stated flatly that he had called because he was already over there and was afraid they would catch him at her house. That's where he had been every night that he said he was working late.

Gracie slid to the floor in disbelief. It was happening again! All Gracie could think of was that it was all her fault. Thoughts flooded her eleven-year-old mind of how her attempt to help this family in their time of need caused her family to fall apart again. Her dad was abandoning her again, and she believed it was all her fault. She thought being a good daughter that didn't cause any trouble would keep him home this time. As it turns out, the plan backfired on her. She wasn't enough.

Then the thought hit her, *Mandy has my dad now! How could this happen!* How could this happen! Gracie withdrew into a shell and nothing could get her out.

That night changed her life forever. No one could have known at the time how her dad's decision would affect her relationship decisions for the next forty-five years.

CHAPTER 5

❦

So Many Changes

It had been a month since the devastating news of Gracie's dad leaving her again. She had such a hard time processing the pain from the first divorce; the second time, it was utterly unbearable with her carrying the guilt of him leaving. As her mom worked hard to regroup and create a new normal for all of them, Gracie could not shake the tormenting thoughts of it being her fault. No matter what her mom or grannie said to comfort her, she couldn't help but carry the blame. Gracie became very insecure; her self-confidence and self-esteem took quite a hit.

While her mom did everything she could to help Gracie get through the first divorce, she needed to be battle ready for what was to come with the second divorce. It would be many years later before Gracie would understand that it wasn't her fault. Her dad never stopped having affairs and would have eventually left for someone had it not been Mandy's mom that he left. What Gracie couldn't know and was too young to understand was that her "perfect" dad was far from perfect. Gracie had no idea the demons tormenting him or that he had countless affairs with other women. Her mother loved him so much and tried to be the best wife so that he wouldn't want to leave, but her best efforts couldn't solve the issues he was dealing with internally.

Not being able to understand this at her young age, she did the only thing she knew to do, and that was to blame herself for bringing Mandy and her family into their lives. While she was beating herself up for tearing her family apart, her health began suffering from the stress of it all.

Her mom no longer had to see Mandy's mom at the office, but Gracie had to go to school and see Mandy every day in class. It was so painful. She just thought Mandy was mean before, something came over Mandy, and she pulled out all the stops to hurt Gracie. The verbal abuse was more than she could take. Gracie had tried so hard to bring joy to Mandy's life. She couldn't understand how Mandy could be so mean to her again after all they had been through together. Gracie's stomach stayed in knots all the time. It was so difficult to deal with the loss of her dad and the abuse from Mandy. Together it was too much for her to bear. She couldn't eat. She was losing weight, and she became very weak. She missed a week of school. When her mom coaxed her into going back to school, Mandy came in that day all excited. She was talking loudly so Gracie could hear her telling the other kids in their class that "her dad" would be taking her and her brother to Disney World. *Her dad?* Gracie thought to herself, *That isn't her dad; that is my dad!* Gracie was devastated. Her dad had never taken her and her brother to Disney World; she couldn't understand why he was taking them. The thoughts of them together and her claiming Gracie's dad as her own, Gracie couldn't breathe.

Gracie's mom was so upset to find out what had happened at school. She could not have been more upset with her ex at that moment but had to keep her focus on helping Gracie. In an attempt to cheer her, her mom surprised her with a poodle puppy that she had always wanted, a puffy white poodle. She was happy to have her; she named her Fluffy. It wasn't enough though; the puppy comforted her, but she still didn't want to go to school and face Mandy.

Gracie's mom took her to the doctor for advice and help as she was still not eating well and getting weaker. He said the only way to help her was to get her away from the problem—the problem being her dad and Mandy. Gracie's mom didn't have a choice but to sell their home, move them across town away from their neighborhood friends, put Gracie in a new school system, and not reveal their whereabouts to their father. It was two years before her mom told him where they lived. When he wanted to see the kids during those two years, she would bring them to her office, and he would have to pick them up from there. Their mom told them not to tell him where they lived. It took Gracie a long time to heal, and her mom was very protective of her, not wanting her dad to stir up her anxiety again. He had a habit of making bad decisions, so she didn't want to risk Gracie's health to satisfy him for a brief visit.

Uprooting their life and moving across town was challenging in so many ways. Mark was fifteen at the time and had a license to drive a motorcycle. He was one of the popular guys at school, played football, and the girls loved him. He had a steady girlfriend at the time and didn't want to leave the life he had created for himself. Their mom had so much on her mind that she allowed him to convince her to let him continue going to his high school. He drove across town every day to school while Gracie got her first taste at riding a school bus to her new school. It was a scary time of change for Gracie, leaving her best friend Camela behind; and just when she needed her comfort pet the most, she had to give her up as they moved into an apartment that didn't allow pets. The doctor's plan was the best course of action for Gracie and set her on a path to recovery, even though it was a long while before she settled into this new life.

The only constant was that they still attended the same church even though they had moved across town. Gracie had friends there that she didn't have to leave and looked forward to going to church every time the doors were opened. Gracie's mom allowed her to do all church activities and camps that she could manage to get her too. Her church family was good for her. Adonai used them to help her get through the horrific season of change for her.

Gracie's dad had no idea how his decisions affected her; abandoning her was eating her alive. She learned many years later that her abandonment issues affected all her relationships as she sabotaged them one by one. It was a miracle that she didn't spiral out of control and get into permanent trouble.

CHAPTER 6

My Bestest Friend

After so many changes in Gracie's life, the sweet, bubbly little girl who loved making people laugh and smile had disappeared for a while. She had withdrawn to her safe place, alone with Adonai. The new Gracie was very guarded and didn't trust anyone with her heart. She assumed all kids would bully her and that no one was a real friend. For a while, when other kids were nice to her, she stayed withdrawn and untrusting, assuming that it wasn't sincere and wouldn't last. It would be a while before she got over what Mandy did to her.

When she met someone she liked, she would be so overly friendly, wanting them to like her that it would drive them away. She fell into a hole socially, unable to make friends. She had no clue who to trust, so she trusted no one. Her popular move was to allow someone to be a friend for a short time and then drive them away before leaving her. As hard as she tried to shut everyone out, she couldn't help but want a true friend.

Gracie's mom was busy working long days trying to provide for all of them but always ensured they were in church. Mark wasn't interested in being at this church with them as he was in his teenage years and wanted to do his own thing with his high school friends. He was five years older than Gracie, so it wasn't like they were close anyway. They were both handling the divorce the best they could. Gracie loved being at church; she found joy there that she had never known before. She was baptized at age five but didn't enjoy going to church until her preteen years. Someone had invited her mom to visit a different church one day, Gracie and her mom loved it. She knew that the kids were exhausted from all the changes. Her mom asked them to go three times with her before they decided if they liked it or not. Gracie loved it! It moved her spirit; she felt at home there. This particular church seemed to be an environment of learning and love that she needed at the time. She wanted to be a good girl and do what was right, but she still couldn't get the relationship part figured out.

She didn't know how to have a relationship with anyone, not even her heavenly Father. She had no examples, no one to teach her. Not that someone couldn't teach her, she didn't know what she needed, so she didn't know how to ask for help. All she could identify with was abandonment, so she learned not to get close to anyone so she wouldn't get hurt again. She finally figured out that if she couldn't have a healthy human relationship, maybe she could find a healthy one with her heavenly Father. It seemed her attempts to get close to Him brought her peace, so she kept working in that direction as best she could to see if that path would give her the answers to which she was searching.

Still going through the motions, trying to find peace and happiness, Gracie felt so utterly alone. It's hard to explain feeling lonely when at the same time you somehow know you are not alone in your pain. The pain was real, her life journey bumpy, but there was some level of inner peace that she couldn't explain. Adonai was with her the whole time, even though she didn't realize it yet.

Like a magnet drawn to metal, Gracie was always ready to go to church; her mom never had to coax her. In her room getting ready, Gracie heard her mom say, "Hurry up, get in the car, or you are going to be late!" Gracie grabbed her things and ran down the steps and jumped in the car. She could hardly wait to see what the teacher had for them to do. This day turned out to be special; there was a new girl in Sunday school class. She was a fun, bubbly girl named Kimmie; she made Gracie laugh. Even though Gracie had been hurt so badly by Mandy and made her withdrawn and untrusting, it was ingrained in Gracie's nature to make everyone feel loved and special. She could not stand for anyone to feel alone or left out.

Whenever there was a new kid in class, she made it her mission to make them feel welcomed. Gracie really liked this girl. She and her family had just moved to town and started going to church there. Gracie couldn't help but want to be friends with her, and she loved her parents and little sister. They invited her to their home often to spend the night; it was so much fun. When Gracie was with them, she pretended they were her happy family. Gracie and Kimmie really enjoyed being together. They loved singing their favorite songs from the top of their lungs, doing gymnastics, and being silly together. If anyone was looking for them, you could usually find them outside doing handstands and cartwheels. Kimmie's dad was the football coach for their church school, so she and Kimmie became cheerleaders and went to all the practices and games to be around the boys. Gracie loved Kimmie's dad. He seemed happy and in love with his wife. He seemed like a great dad and played with all of them whenever she was over. He was so fun to be around. It made her happy to be around with their family. Gracie wanted to hang out with Kimmie and her family as often as her mom would let her. They were inseparable for two years. She had invited Kimmie over one particular night and had planned for them to stay up all night being silly.

When Kimmie got to the apartment, she didn't seem like herself. Her parents were talking to Gracie's mom as they went into Gracie's room. She asked Kimmie what was wrong. She said that her dad had been offered a job back home, three states away, and would be moving at the end of the school year. Gracie stared in disbelief. Did she hear her correctly? Is she dreaming? There is no way her best friend is abandoning her. No, no, no! As her thoughts raced, trying to process what was happening, Gracie couldn't stop the tears that began running down her face; her heart ached. Kimmie cried herself to sleep, but Gracie couldn't sleep that night. Gracie stared up at the glowing stars stuck to the ceiling of her bedroom and wondered how she was going to convince her mom to let her move with Kimmie and her family. Gracie couldn't remember a happier time in her life than when they were together. She finally drifted off to sleep with no solution to her problem. After that night, Gracie was so sad that Kimmie was leaving; it was impossible to enjoy her last days in town. Gracie did what she had learned to do for years, withdraw and shut everyone out. She made a promise to herself that night that she would not be able to keep, to never to let anyone in her heart again.

CHAPTER 7

Summers with Dad

By the time Gracie was entering middle school, it had appeared that time and her years seeking Adonai did so much in helping her heal. Gracie was learning that she could trust Adonai, even though she still didn't trust people. Slowly each event of someone she cared about abandoning her caused her to lose her self-esteem and self-confidence a little more each time.

Her dad was in a place where he thought he was settled with his current family and wanted to reach out and invite her to his beach house with them for the summer. Gracie had been separated from them for so many years that she could better deal with seeing them by the time she was in middle school.

While losing her dad in her everyday life was devastatingly challenging all those years ago, she was in stunned disbelief to learn that it wasn't her only loss. When he married Mandy's mom, Gracie's dad's mom announced that she and Mark were no longer her grandkids. She said that Mandy and her brother had taken their places in her life. Their grandmother had abandoned them as well. Gracie didn't know how to process that statement. She thought to herself, *Maybe that was normal. Maybe that is what people were supposed to do in a divorce.* Gracie didn't have anything to compare it to, so she told herself, "This is life, deal with it."

Making an effort with her dad and his family, Gracie agreed to accept his invitation. At this age, Mandy was bearable. Gracie knew Mandy had gone through battles of her own over the years; Gracie was not the same person either, so they called a truce and decided to be sisters. What she discovered spending summers with Mandy is that she had spiraled out of control through the years. Both Gracie and Mandy spent their childhood searching for acceptance and happiness. Gracie found what she needed in a relationship with her heavenly Father; Mandy sought it through boys and drugs.

Once she realized Mandy was not doing well, Gracie felt Adonai had sent her to help her sister. That wasn't to say that Gracie had all the answers or had it all figured out, not at all. Adonai had healed her in many ways and carried her through the worst storms of her life. But she still had so many scars and healing areas of her own.

Gracie still believed it wasn't possible to trust anyone with her heart and had inadvertently turned into a people pleaser somewhere along the way. She became obsessed with what others thought of her. Gracie couldn't help but try to get people to like her. Her mode of operation had not changed. If they seemed to like her, she would sabotage the relationship before they could hurt her. It didn't always work, but usually, she was out before the other person.

Even with her troubles, she felt like she needed to take the high road with Mandy and see how she could help. The first summer together wasn't too bad. She pretended to be a local with them and learned what the locals do every afternoon. Some days, they would sit and watch the boats come in and see what the catch of the day was, which was always super fun to see the catch and watch them weigh and clean them. Other days they would watch the sunset from the docks while socializing; some days, there was a sunset boat ride, or they would sit around the pool and enjoy chatting with neighbors while eating unlimited raw oysters. Some of the men that lived there would bring in several ten-gallon buckets full of oysters to share with everyone. There were lots of crackers and hot cocktail sauce involved as well. Unlimited oysters, isn't that the way they get served at restaurants? Gracie thought it was disgusting when she first saw them. Her dad patiently taught her to eat them right out of the shell on a cracker with cocktail sauce. She was surprised at how delicious they were. Before she knew it, she had eaten almost two dozen herself. It was a fun bonding time with her dad. Her brother was living there that summer after his high school graduation.

A jolly older man named Mr. Stan lived next door to her dad, who loved to bake fresh sourdough bread. His son would be there often for a visit as well. His name was Stan Jr. Mr. Stan Sr. looked like the Pillsbury doughboy to her, but he was bald and much older. When Gracie would smell him cooking bread, she would lean over the balcony to his balcony and call out to Mr. Stan to see when it would be ready. It made him so happy that she was excited about his bread; it gave him purpose to see her smile. Everyone loved his bread. She wanted to be first before it was gone. Mr. Stan always brought it out to share with lots of butter. It was never enough, and she wished she didn't have to share. But it was probably a good thing; otherwise, she would have gone home at the end of the summer ten pounds heavier.

It was fun to have someone to go to the beach with every day. Mandy and Gracie loved to lay out in the sun and walk the beach; it was also fun to look at the cute boys together. One day, they had a bright idea to go to the beach in their bathing suits, not taking anything with them, no towels, no cover-ups, flip-flops, sunscreen, or water. That way, they would be free to walk the beach and not have to worry about keeping up with their stuff. It turned out to be a very bad idea. Gracie had very sensitive feet and had not factored in walking or running down the scorching pavement in the alley behind the condo across from them to get to the beach. They made it to the beach, but their feet blistered from the hot pavement. It wasn't long before they realized that they needed all of the things that they left behind. The summer turned out pretty well, considering it was her first time to see them in five years.

The following summer didn't turn out as well. It started okay, but it seemed like Mandy was struggling. She was preoccupied and seemed to have changed a lot since the summer before. One night, she wanted to walk the beach to go to a bonfire some friends were having. Gracie quickly discovered that it wasn't a bonfire but three guys with "pot" sitting around a fire they made to get "high" with them; Mandy hadn't told Gracie the truth. Gracie told them she wasn't interested. They made fun of her for not wanting to smoke with them, calling her a chicken and other names. Gracie was used to people bullying her, and it would always hurt her feelings. Not this time, she was confident about her decision. One of them said, "don't you want to get high?" She responded by telling them that she was on a "natural high." They looked at her with a blank stare, having no clue what she meant. The "high" they were looking for, Gracie found in a relationship with her heavenly Father. What they couldn't understand in their current state of mind was that her "natural high" would last for eternity. No one knew that recently, Gracie had a personal encounter with the Holy Spirit, and she chose to give her life to Him and completely trust Adonai to take care of her (Joshua 24:15, Galatians 2:20, Luke 1:35). She had a new boldness and courage that she had never experienced before (Acts 4:31). Knowing that she was not alone, her heavenly Father was with her, protecting her, watching over her, and giving her indescribable courage. While they smoked around the fire pit, Gracie walked the beach alone in the moonlight, talking to the one and only that truly knew her inside and out, her heavenly Father.

It came as no surprise that this summer didn't seem to go as smoothly as the last one. Gracie observed that her dad and Mandy's mom didn't seem happy either. Mandy said they fight all the time, and she couldn't handle it; that's why she wanted to stay stoned.

One night, when Gracie and Mandy were asleep on the bottom level of the townhouse, they were suddenly awakened in the night by screaming and the sound of things breaking. They ran upstairs and found their parents fighting. Standing there, not believing her eyes, Gracie was frozen, watching them scream at each other, not knowing what to do. Her dad turned and saw her standing there and started toward her. He grabbed her hand and said, "Let's go." When she asked him what was going on, he told her that they were getting a divorce. Gracie didn't know how to respond or how she felt about it. Divorce was her normal. So it didn't surprise her, nor did it have the same effect on her as it did when he left her all those years ago. She wondered if she was glad or sad about it. Did she care? The only thing she was sure about was her love for her dad. She knew he wasn't perfect, but she still adored him—imperfections, bad decisions, and all. As long as she could be with him, she didn't care whom he married.

Gracie and her dad spent the night on his thirty-foot boat docked behind the townhouse complex as they lived on the canal. The next day they got up, and she helped him get his things together. Gracie knew then why Mandy had been acting so strange all summer; she knew it was coming. Gracie hugged Mandy goodbye. Then she and her dad left for him to drive her back home to Alabama. Gracie never saw them again. Her brother Mark stayed down there working and was invited to stay on a family's yacht that he had befriended. At the end of the summer, he then traveled back to Houston with that family to start a new work career they offered him. Their dad approved of the move since it was a great opportunity for Mark.

When they got back to town, her dad stayed to talk and visit with Gracie's mom. She didn't know what they talked about, but she noticed a change in her mom. Gracie observed that her mom was happier and willing to let her dad come around, particularly during the holidays. Gracie didn't have any expectations; she was just glad to have him around and see a smile on her mom's face. It was hard to tell if her dad was happy to be around them during the holidays; he seemed to have a lot on his mind. Regardless, Gracie was so excited to have him around as much as possible. Who knew how long it would last?

He never moved back to town and was rarely around after the holidays. On the rare occasions Gracie got to see him, it was great. Her love for him never waned, nor did her disappointment that he chose other women over her. She was grateful for any time that he decided to spend with her.

Not long after the holidays, they found out he had found a new girlfriend. Gracie thought about her dad and how sad he appeared with or without a girlfriend. He seemed to be searching for someone who could make his pain go away, not realizing that only Adonai makes that happen. She often prayed her dad would find what he was searching for and recognize that peace can only come from one source. After his divorce to Mandy's mom, Gracie's dad's mother reached out to let her and her brother know that they were once again her grandchildren now that he was divorced. Both were stunned and didn't know how to respond to that announcement. After all those years apart, it was impossible for Gracie and Mark to trust her with their heart again. Since Gracie loved her dad so much, she made an effort to connect with her grandmother, but sadly there was never a bond between them again.

Gracie's brother had already graduated high school and moved away to start a life of his own. She and her brother fought a lot, as siblings do, and Gracie could hardly wait for the day for him to graduate and move away. When the day arrived, Gracie wasn't sure that was what she wanted. Now things weren't going great at home with Gracie and her mom after her dad left again. There were huge disagreements about how Gracie should feel about her dad abandoning them again. It seemed the only hope for either of them to get through this difference of opinion was for Gracie to move out. She spent her entire freshman year of high school living with her aunt, uncle, and cousin, Jules. Gracie was so grateful for their generosity to let her live with them. The year apart helped her and her mom recover from their disagreements. Gracie moved home before her sophomore year with the determination to live at peace with her mom.

CHAPTER 8

My Endless Love

In the summer before her junior year in high school, Gracie fell head over heels in love with a guy at church named Beau, a cute guy in the youth group. Since being so involved at her church and working on her relationship with Adonai, she softened a bit and began learning to trust others with her heart. Then she met Beau. He was a year older than her and a senior in high school. They dated for a year; it was the happiest she had been since Kimmie moved away many years before. She had finally found happiness in dating someone that made her laugh and seemed to care about her. Her favorite moments with him were when they would sing the Lionel Ritchie and Diana Ross's "Endless Love" duet together at the top of their lungs in the car driving down the road, holding hands. She enjoyed their time together, laughing and having fun; she loved him so much. He could make her forget about all of her problems. She knew they would marry one day and that she would never have to worry about him abandoning her. He was her everything.

Gracie's mom liked him fine and was happy for them to date as long as she kept her grades up. She spent lots of time with his large family; he had nine siblings. Gracie pretended they were her siblings too; she couldn't believe how blessed she was to find this true love. When she wasn't at school or work, she was hanging out at their house. Gracie's mom was glad that she was finally happy.

Summer vacations were coming to an end, and it was time for school to start. They had been through so much together, good and bad, the bad being the death of his father who tragically died of a heart attack at work. She was glad to be there for him during that difficult time. Now it was going to be Gracie's senior year of high school. She could hardly wait to get through the year and graduate so that she and Beau could get married, just one more year. This time of year also meant it was time for Beau to head off to college; he was moving to a Florida campus. Gracie was struggling, but he promised that he would call often and come home as much as possible. Before cell phones or computers to FaceTime or talk existed, they depended on landlines to stay in touch. Beau called Gracie the first couple of weeks. Then when he called next, something was different. He missed a week calling her, and Gracie had an uneasy feeling in her spirit; she would soon learn she had a reason to be worried. Gracie was at his mom's house hanging out with his mom and his sisters as she did as often as possible; it was her happy place. The phone rang, and it was her "endless love" on the other end. She was so excited! She excitedly grabbed the phone from his mom and just beamed when she heard his voice. It was almost as if she held her breath the whole week until they spoke. Thoughts of him kept her motivated to get through the week until the next call. She was blissful as she listened to him talk about how things were going at school. Gracie was excited for him and wanted him to share every detail. While she was riding high on the excitement of his call and could hear his sisters laughing and cutting up in the next room, she barely noticed when his tone changed in the conversation.

He said, "Hey, I have something I need to tell you." Gracie waited to hear what it could be that changed his tone so drastically. What did the love of her life have to say to her that sounded so serious? He proceeded to explain to her how much fun he was having and then added, "There are so many beautiful girls down here. I had no idea it would be like this."

"Wait! What? What are you saying?"

He said, "I think we need to take a break until I can figure out what I want."

All the color left Gracie's face. One of his sisters walked into the kitchen to get something out of the refrigerator. She noticed the change in Gracie's countenance. Gracie's head was spinning. How could this be happening again? She let someone in her heart. She trusted him explicitly. She fell hard for him. They had talked about getting married. How could this be happening? Beau had just announced that he was abandoning their relationship so nonchalantly. He didn't seem to care how it affected her at the moment. Even though he knew what she had been through, he was so giddy. All he could talk about were his new girlfriend prospects. It was such a surprise announcement blindsiding her that she went into shock. She didn't know what to say.

One of Beau's sisters took the phone from her as she sat there stunned in a stare trying to process what she had heard. He said something to his sister, and she hung the phone up. His mom and sisters all came running in and asked what had happened. She told them what he said. They were stunned. As the initial shock began to subside, Gracie could hear them chatting with each other about what had happened. Suddenly Gracie saw herself as an outsider to this family; she realized she was no longer one of them. Immediately her heart began to withdraw for safety into the zone of trusting no one again—male, female, young, old, preacher, teacher, no one. She had to make changes to get away from the pain again.

From the first time her dad left her, the most effective way to help Gracie was to remove her from the problem. Her first love's abandonment hit her as hard as when her dad left and Kimmie moved away. All of those feelings of loss came flooding back in to fill the spot in her heart that was momentarily full of joy.

CHAPTER 9

Amy to the Rescue

During her year with Beau and when the breakup occurred, Gracie's mom had her hands full dealing with personal health issues that she had not shared with her. Gracie spent so little time at home due to school, work, and hanging out with Beau and his family that she and her mom didn't see much of each other. Her mom was working full-time running her own business while attending college classes at night when her health took a turn. Gracie was happy when her mom told her that she was going to attend night college classes. She was happy and wanted her mom to be happy too. Her mom was finally getting to do something for herself. When she started her college journey, her mom never would have dreamed that her body would betray her. She knew it wouldn't be long before Gracie graduated high school and then possibly move on to marry Beau and start a new life. She didn't want to disrupt Gracie's happiness and tell her what was going on in her life. At that time, Gracie didn't have a clue that her "endless love" was about to betray her.

Gracie was so devastated by the breakup. She didn't know what to do with the heaviness weighing on her. It was that time again. She needed to get away from everything and everyone that reminded her of loss in her life; she shared her situation with Amy, her best friend in high school. Fortunately, Gracie and her mom still lived across town from their church, so she didn't have to see anyone from the church unless she drove across town to see them. After talking, Amy had a great idea and said she should come live with her. Amy went home and asked her mom if Gracie could move in with them. She was an only child and always wanted to have a sister; her parents agreed to let her stay as long as both kept their grades up. Expecting her mom to say no, Gracie practiced her best speech yet. To her surprise, her mom agreed. She didn't have to beg, cry, or debate; she said okay. Gracie was surprised but excited.

Gracie had no idea that her mom agreed to let her move out her senior year because she didn't want Gracie to worry about her possibly fatal cancer diagnosis she had received and be concerned about her abandoning Gracie too. Her mom had gone to her yearly checkup and seemed to have a good visit, but a few months later, she discovered a lump on her breast. In that short amount of time between the doctor's visit and finding the lump was a quick growth and had affected several lymph nodes, the prognosis was uncertain.

It seemed that things had worked out with perfect timing for Amy's invitation for Gracie to stay with her for a while. Hopefully all would go well, and there would be nothing for her to worry about. Her mom's best friend moved in to take care of her. Gracie thought her mom just wanted to rent a room to help offset expenses; she was happy for her mom not to be alone. It seemed like it was a win-win for both of them.

Gracie was super excited and immediately moved out and started going to church with Amy and her parents. It was such a relief to her to try to move forward and build a new life without Beau. It wasn't her first time to deal with painful change and would most likely not be her last. It was time to move on. She knew that Adonai would help her do this and that it would take time for her to heal.

She loved going to Amy's church; she didn't know a soul there and could be herself and not worry about anyone knowing what she had just been through with Beau. They all made her feel so welcomed. There were many cute guys in the youth group with ages ranging from eighteen to twenty-eight. It helped her feelings and aided in her healing to know that there were guys flirting with her. Where Beau had made her question her self-worth, these new guy friends at church made her feel special. This attention was not improper, and most of them turned out to be friends only, like big brothers. One guy stepped up and asked her out. He was cute, already out of high school with a good job. Gracie was flattered that he asked her out. They went out about three or four times, but Gracie discovered real quick that they didn't have anything in common. There was no spark. He was a nice guy, just not the one for her.

She knew there was hope for healing and happiness somewhere down the road because Adonai always took care of her. Through all her pain, she still believed that her heavenly Father was with her every step. His Word doesn't say life will be easy; it says He will always be with us and protect us (John 16:33). She knew she was in a safe place with Adonai and was ready for the next chapter in her life—next step, the one right behind Adonai, following His lead.

CHAPTER 10

Laughter Is the Best Medicine

Gracie wasn't looking for a relationship; she was looking for joy and peace and to forget about Beau. Gracie and Amy went to the youth group socials; Gracie enjoyed their time together. It was good for her after Beau had broken her heart and shattered her dreams of them being together. Beau had abandoned her without hesitation, just like her dad did so many years before.

Being brave and trusting her heavenly Father to take care of her, Gracie focused on moving forward (Philippians 4:13). She had decided that from now on, when she decided to date, it would be with someone older and more stable; she felt that guys her age were silly and immature.

Even in her sadness from the breakup, she still loved to laugh and cut up, but someone had to be unique to snap her out of her funk. It turned out there was a guy at church that had this special talent. He was funny and loved singing and playing the guitar; he led the singing at church and at their gatherings. She was always fascinated by those who could sing and play musical instruments, forever regretting that it never worked out for her to have the opportunity to learn piano from a good teacher. That dream of playing piano died many, many years ago, and she never dared ask again if she could take lessons. In her mind, she believed she was a quitter, so she never tried to start any hobbies.

Watching Gary play the guitar at the church socials was fun. His personality was infectious. He had a great voice, and he made her laugh. As a bonus, Gary was ten years older than Gracie. She tried not to let him in her heart, but he had all the right personality traits to get her attention. When she was least expecting it, he had her laughing so hard that she was crying. Gracie couldn't remember ever laughing so hard; he made her forget her problems when they were together. They ended up hanging out together at all the socials and laughing together constantly. His bubbly personality was infectious. Nothing else mattered when they were together; he kept her laughing, which greatly distracted her from her pain. She thought to herself, *He's perfect for me. Funny, talented, loves our heavenly Father, and he's older and more stable than the guys her age.* They were an unlikely match to those who knew them both, but he made her happy. Gracie wanted happiness; she wanted someone who "wanted" to be with her forever. She wanted to be chosen and cherished by someone. Gracie knew Adonai adored her, but she told Him repeatedly that she needed a human to love her too. She prayed, "Can this be the one?"

Gracie's senior year flew by thanks to Amy and Gary keeping her too busy to think about her breakup. It turned out to be a decent year. Gracie was trying to decide what to do after graduation. She didn't ask if she could go to college. Gracie knew her mom couldn't afford it, and it was a lot of money for her to request as a quitter. During career day at school, she had entertained the idea of becoming a flight attendant. She was super excited about it because she could work and travel all over the world. With this idea, her mom wouldn't have to pay anything for her to go. What could be better? Everyone else would be at college for four years, studying all day, while she would be traveling the world. In her mind, she already pictured herself in the job. With great anticipation, Gracie filled out the paperwork and sent it in. When she received a response letter in the mail, she was so excited she couldn't breathe as she was about to open it. And just like that, her heart sank while reading the rejection letter. They had turned her down because she did not meet the height requirements. At the time, it was a requirement to be at least

5'3"; Gracie was only 5'. Dreams dashed. Time for a plan B. What would that be? It was frustrating that everything she wanted to do would not work out.

Gracie didn't want to go back home and live with her mom after being at Amy's all year, and she didn't have any good job opportunities. Her parents were encouraging her to move to Florida for the summer with her dad and his current girlfriend, working as his secretary for the summer. There were no other options for her at the time. This plan of theirs would also get her away from the current guy in her life.

By the time Gracie was graduating high school, her dad had been with so many different women that she stopped trying to meet them; they would be gone as quickly as she met them. The idea of going to live with him and his girlfriend seemed like a good plan because it was probably a short-term relationship for him anyway. He was excited for her to come down, so she was packing up to head that way. Before she left, Gary surprised her and proposed. She was so excited! They talked and agreed for her to go ahead to the beach to work for the summer as planned, and they would make wedding plans long distance.

Gracie was unaware that her mom was working with her dad behind her back to break off the engagement. Her mom knew that if anyone could convince her to break off the engagement, it would be her dad that she adored. After long face-to-face conversations with her dad, he persuaded her to call off the wedding engagement. Her parents had convinced her that he was wrong for her.

At the end of the summer, Gracie moved back to Alabama. Beach living was not for her; the summer was all she could take. After moving back to town and finding a place of her own and a new job, Gracie decided to return to her old church again. Beau was still away at college, and enough time had passed that she felt like it was safe to go back to the church home that she loved. Gary helped her get past the pain of her breakup with Beau, and the split with Gary didn't hit her as hard; apparently, her parents were right. If she had been as crazy about him as she was Beau, she wouldn't have agreed to break up with him so easily. It was time for a new chapter.

CHAPTER 11

Telling God My Plan

Gracie had dated guys from church or gone on blind dates, but none which warranted a second date. A handsome policeman in his upper twenties asked her out for a bit, and she really liked him until she found out he was married. Gracie was horrified when she found out and broke things off with him in spite of his begging not to end things. Her best friend at church had a cute, fun brother named Wayne that was a few years old than she was, and she had a crush on him for a bit. He played the piano and sang; she loved to watch him play. They began dating and had been for a little while when he had this bright idea that he would take a shot at going to the college where Beau was attending. It was a Christian college that many from their church went to after high school. Wayne was in his midtwenties and had a chance to go and was excited.

He said, "Let's take a break for a while until I get back."

Gracie said, "Yeah, let's do that," as she rolled her eyes.

Gracie let him go in her heart as soon as he said he was going to that college. He said, "Don't fall in love with anyone. Just date."

"Uh-huh", she responded.

Gracie had already been down this path. He knew that because she told him the whole story. Curiosity must have gotten the best of Wayne; he needed to check out Beau's story and see if it was true, insert another eye roll. At this point, Gracie didn't care. She was disappointed, but she figured he wasn't the one.

Believing that everyone met their spouse at college, Gracie knew she was at a disadvantage not attending herself. Since she couldn't go to college, she was determined to marry a guy from her church group. The first two didn't work out, but God must have one for her in that group. Surely there was a special someone for her there that would adore her and never want to leave her. She had so much love to give to that special someone if she could just find him. Gracie didn't want to be alone.

Gracie never missed a church social. She always enjoyed them, but she was on a mission to find a husband. There was one guy that she had been eyeing for a while. One night, the college and career pastor preached a great message on "how to find your soul mate." Gracie was intent on getting the details so that she could make it work for her. What she heard the pastor say was, "Tell God who you want, and he will give you the desires of your heart." What he actually said was "pray about the qualities you want in a spouse, and God will give you the desires of your heart." She was listening so intently that she heard what she wanted to hear. At the end of his message, he had everyone write down what came to mind; then he had them bow their heads and pray about it. Most wrote down qualities. Gracie wrote a name over and over on her piece of paper. She then bowed her head with one eye open as she turned and looked straight at the guy she thought would be perfect for her and told God, "That's who I want. I want Jimmy." He was cute, only a year older than her, and had a decent job. She felt like her mom would approve of this one.

That had to be one of many moments when God shook His head, knowing that she had missed the point of the message. That twenty-year-old guy had no idea what his nineteen-year-old friend Gracie had just done. She set her sights on him and was determined he would marry her because she told God that's who she wanted, and He was going to give her the desires of her heart. She set out to work her plan without talking to anyone about it, not even God (Genesis 16:2). She believed God would do what the pastor said he would do, so she needed to do her part to help God make it happen (Proverbs

16:9). Oh boy, what a slippery slope people find themselves on when they tell God what to do and then help Him do it their way. When people are persistent in their plan and do not ask Him what His plan is for them, He will often let them figure it out the hard way. Jimmy slowly came around to her way of thinking, and they began dating. They spent a lot of time together and got along well. Gracie was determined to make this work.

Funny sidebar: Gracie and Jimmy went to a church party one night, and she was excitedly telling everyone about their engagement. She heard people whispering about something, so she turned to see what they were discussing. Gracie looked toward a group of people talking. When they parted, she saw a familiar face across the room that she had not seen in a long time; it was Wayne. He was back from college. He had decided that it wasn't for him and wanted to surprise her. She had not heard from him since he left the year before. She walked over and said hello and welcomed him back. He said he came back to surprise her, but he got his own surprise. Gracie reminded him that he said they were going to date other people. He said, "Yeah, but you weren't supposed to get engaged." Gracie giggled at the logic. He shrugged and walked off. She was so glad she didn't sit around pining for him.

Looking back many years later, Gracie could see a million red flags to get off the crazy train she was on trying to make the wedding with Jimmy happen, but Gracie ignored them all. One huge indicator that this plan was not a good one was he didn't want to get married. He didn't ask her to marry him, she asked him. Another big indicator was her mom was totally against her marrying him; she had a list of reasons. She said, "Nothing against him, but he is not the one for you." It had come to the point in their relationship over the years and especially since she was nineteen and didn't have to do what her mom told her to do that when her mom gave her a direct order without listening to her side of the story, Gracie was going to do it her way even if it killed her. Since her mother shot down the marriage to Gary, she decided her mom was being difficult. She felt like she was battling this to punish her for something. Gracie felt like she wanted her to be alone, so she defied her order and went on with her plan.

After a year of dating, he finally agreed to marry her, but he insisted the engagement be a year. She had talked him into getting married; that was an exhausting process in itself. If he wanted the engagement to be a year, she planned to spend it busy getting ready for the big day. She had won half the battle; she decided to let him win that one. At least there was a date set. Her plan was finally going to happen, and she was confident he wasn't going to back out because, in her mind, God had promised her that she could have him. Her fear of abandonment caused her to go overboard trying to control the situation. It was people-pleasing mode on steroids. What must he have been thinking to allow this? Looking back, she thought, *Would he have ever asked her on his own?* They both had reasons for agreeing to this arrangement; sadly, they did not build their relationship on love.

Gracie thought it was a win-win for both of them. He wanted to get out of his house living at home with his parents and brother, and she wanted to get married, have someone to love her. He had gone straight to a full-time job after high school as well. Gracie planned to spoil him so that he wouldn't be able to resist loving her so much that he would think he had won the jackpot by marrying her. As Julia Roberts said in the movie *Pretty Woman*, "Baby, I'm going to treat you so good that you are never going to want to let me go." That was her plan, to win him over by being the best wife ever.

Warning, big obstacle ahead! One of the drawbacks of proceeding with her plan without her mom's blessing was that she would not pay for the wedding. She was already upset that Gracie had asked her dad to give her away at the wedding. Her mom felt that he had given her away many years ago when he left and had no right to that honor at her wedding. The fact that he abandoned Gracie more than once and didn't pay child support, then to get that honor while not helping pay for the wedding, was not going to happen on her dime. They had to postpone their wedding date for a few months until they could come up with an alternate plan to pay for it themselves, but Gracie was dead set on getting married; nothing was going to stop her. She couldn't understand why her mom was so determined to prevent her from being happy.

Gracie determined that nothing was going to stop her dad from walking her down the aisle on her special day. It was important to her. With her mom not funding the wedding, she couldn't call the shots anymore, so the wedding went on as Gracie had planned. She was going to win this battle! She would get married to Jimmy that day.

Since Gracie had ignored all God's warnings to not go this path, against Him and without His blessing, there was no way for Gracie to see all the looming problems on the other side of "I do." As one would expect when the mom says no and God says no, to push through anyway only spells disaster for all parties. Any plan that is not God's plan for one's life is not going to end well (Jeremiah 29:11).

CHAPTER 12

The Wedding

The *big* day had arrived! Gracie's plan was coming together. Thunderstorms and a tornado watch overhead did not deter Gracie in any way. She stayed laser-focused on her goal for her wedding day. She was not going to allow the weather to alter her plan to marry Jimmy. Her dad knocked on the door and asked if she was ready. Her best friend from her childhood that she had to leave behind when they moved across town after the divorce, Camela, was her maid of honor. She helped Gracie get ready, and with the finishing touches done, she looked at Gracie and smiled as she opened the door to let Gracie's dad enter as she exited to head down the aisle. The veil on and adjusted, she stepped out with her something old, new, borrowed, and blue and ecstatically reached for her dad's arm. He was so handsome in his tux. She was excited to walk down the aisle together. As Camela went ahead, Gracie's dad leaned down to kiss her cheek and tell her how much he loved her.

He said, "Are you sure you want to do this? It's not too late to back out."

She giggled. "Daddy, this was my plan. This is what I want."

He said, "If you are sure, let's do this then."

Her heart beamed with love for him; she was so glad he was there. As they began to walk, Gracie suddenly had this horrible feeling come over her. "No, no, no, no, no, no, no, not now!" she said to herself. Gracie knew that her pill schedule showed she could start any day but was praying it would wait until after the wedding. With the music playing and a look of horror on her face with thoughts racing through her head of what going ahead down the aisle might look like in her white dress, she told her dad she had to go back. With a flushed face, she frantically asked him to tell them to give her a few minutes.

Crisis averted, Gracie ran back to her dad waiting in the hall-way; she smiled, and he said, "Are you ready?"

Flushed with embarrassment, she said yes.

Back on his arm, music playing again, off they went. Surely everyone thought she was like Julia Roberts in the *Runaway Bride*. When she rounded the corner to go through the doorway, she couldn't help but notice that Jimmy was as white as his white tux. Not knowing what was going on, was he wondering if she had left him at the altar?

That was the first of many things that went wrong during the wedding. With determination, Gracie got them past all the obstacles. Car packed, clothes changed, bouquet thrown, they were in the car and on the road for a magical honeymoon in the mountains. When they got to their first stop to eat; Gracie said, "Wait, where's my purse?" Jimmy just looked at her with a blank stare. He was supposed to make sure everything made it into the car. Her purse had all their cash in it.

Immediately she found a telephone in the restaurant, and she called her mom. She had noticed her purse was left behind and awaited her call. She asked her mom to overnight to the hotel. Yet another crisis diverted. The list was continually growing. On their drive to Gatlinburg, they were still dodging storms and tornadoes. With each obstacle, Gracie kept a positive attitude. She kept say-ing, "It's okay, no big deal. I'll fix it. Things will get better." But the problems continued. It was like the Whac-A-Mole game. Every time you hit one, another one pops up. The honeymoon turned out to be a bust; so many things went wrong that they decided to go home a day early. They had a long talk before they came home, and he said he didn't want anything in his life to change. He wanted to still do what he wanted to do when he wanted to do it; he enjoyed fishing and hunting with his buddies. She promised him that nothing would change and that she promised to be the perfect wife, and they would be very happy. Unfortunately, she was unable to keep her promises to the unreasonable request. Truth is, everything was going to change, and there was nothing either of them could do about it. The problems continued to mount once they got home. Their marriage was built without a spiritual foundation and with no unified plan from Adonai.

Gracie's efforts to be the perfect wife did not go as planned. Their marriage immediately began to unravel. All her plans and efforts were backfiring on her. While her husband had his issues he needed to work through, Gracie was on track to unintentionally sabotage yet another relationship. She believed that if she couldn't make him blissfully happy with her that he would leave her, and she did not want to be divorced. She didn't want anyone else to leave her. Gracie put unreasonable expectations on her husband to meet all her needs; he couldn't have possibly lived up to them. She was most likely smothering him, trying to be the perfect wife. Was that why he went to his mom's for a visit every night after dinner? He complained daily about her dinner that she worked so hard to cook after working all day. He told her before they got married that he wanted to get away from his mom's house. After they got married, he went over there every night after a failed dinner just to get away from her.

Everything was unraveling. Her husband was supposed to be her protector, her provider, and her best friend. When they were dating, he had told her that his family was wealthy, and they had a mountain home and a beach home. He led her to believe that he was more than capable of taking care of her. He seemed like the perfect guy for her. Surely Adonai was giving her the prince charming she had always needed and wanted, riding in on his white horse to save her from a life of abandonment and fill a life void of love, even though he wasn't the older man in her dreams. How was she to know that his own insecurities caused him to tell her things that weren't true? Gracie put all her trust in Jimmy instead of Adonai. In her desperation to be married, Gracie chose to ignore all the red flags Adonai was showing her not to take this path. She had no idea the consequences to come for ignoring His signs and guidance.

It would be years before she would learn that only her heavenly Father could meet all her needs, not a human (Genesis 15:1). Even when people make mistakes, Adonai still loves His children; His grace is sufficient (2 Corinthians 12:9). Out of all her mistakes in the relationship with Jimmy, Adonai still blessed her. He never misses an opportunity to turn negatives into positives (Romans 8:28). In this case, three years into their marriage, Adonai began blessing them with children. First came Phillip, then fifteen months later came Caroline. They were her life and brought her such joy in the midst of her pain.

It had been an exhausting couple of years since the wedding trying to make her marriage perfect, but this was a special day. The year before she became pregnant with Phillip, Gracie was excited about her dad's rare impending visit to Birmingham. It was April, and her birthday was in a few days. He was coming for a visit; she was so excited that she could hardly wait. She needed to see her dad. Her wedding was the last time he had been to town except for a very brief stop with his brother just three weeks before when their grandmother unexpectedly died. They had driven through for the funeral and stopped to see her for about an hour. It was such a great visit it made her so happy to see both of them; she just wished it had been longer. He had promised that they would spend more time together on this visit as he was on his way to spend time with his mom after her mom's passing.

It had been years since she had spent any quality time with him. Then the past summer, he had invited her and her husband, along with her brother and his wife, down to the beach for the weekend. It was the first ever family vacation with her dad, her brother, and herself since he left them. It was the best vacation ever to hear Gracie tell the story because her dad's idea was to bring them all together. Even though his current girlfriend was with them, it didn't spoil the trip. The only thing that would have made it perfect was to have their mom there. That ship had sailed, so Gracie just focused on the vacation. She couldn't remember having a more perfect time. She and

Jimmy didn't fight that weekend; everyone laughed and had a good time. Gracie did not want the long weekend to end. All of them went to the beach for walks and hanging out, went to the pool, swam, cooked out, played cards, and went to the water park.

The day they went to the water park began as a great day. Gracie was twenty-two and had never been to a water park before. She was so excited and scared to try the slide but was even more excited that her dad was doing it with her. After getting settled and getting their mats, they started up the mountain for what she hoped to be the first of many slides. She and her dad laughed and acted silly all the way up the mountain. Gracie felt like a kid again; he was going to slide with her. She was in heaven, and as they walked up the steps, she thought to herself that it was the best day of her life; she knew nothing could ruin it.

As they got to the top, Gracie's giggles stopped as she saw how high they were. She suddenly got nervous as she had a slight fear of heights. Her dad tried to calm her fears and then suggested that he go first to show her how to do it. Seconds later, all the joy left her body. As her 6'2", 230-pound gorgeous dad put his mat down, the flowing water pulled it from his hand, and it started going down the slide before he could get on it. Gracie's heart leaped in her chest and was immediately horrified as she stood frozen while she watched her dad slip, trying to catch his mat, fall, hit his head, and immediately go sliding down out of control. She reacted without thinking and jumped on her mat right away to get down quickly to catch up and help him.

There was no way to know if he was conscious or injured. Gracie prayed all the way down the slide for Adonai to help him. It seemed like it took forever to get down the slide when it was in reality less than a minute. If someone was watching, they might have sworn they saw Gracie fly off the slide without landing or going under the water. Her goal was to get to her dad as quickly as possible to check on him. *Wait! Where was he?* she asked herself as she desperately searched the pool either for his smile looking for her or a floating body. There were so many people in the water. She was frantically looking in every direction for him when she spotted his body surrounded by a group of laughing kids paying no attention. Gracie got to him as fast as she could, grabbed his body, and turned him over as quickly as possible, crying out, "Dad, Dad, are you okay?" Gracie got no response; he was unconscious. She screamed for help, and the lifeguard immediately came running.

There happened to be paramedics there already; they quickly ran over. While Gracie told them what happened, his girlfriend saw the commotion; she and Gracie's brother, his wife, and her husband came running. The girlfriend told the paramedics that he had heart issues and had glycerin in the glove box in the truck. As she ran to get it, they did CPR and got him revived. Gracie was horrified and relieved that he was going to be okay. Her day did not turn out as she planned; nearly losing her dad and saving her dad's life was not on her list of activities for the day. Now the secret he had been keeping was out; he still had heart issues.

The year before this incident, Gracie received a call that her dad had suffered a heart attack and was in the hospital. She immediately jumped in the car and drove down five hours to check on him. He was in good spirits and said the doctor told him he was going to be just fine. Gracie and her brother had no idea that he had been lying about his health.

After the water park incident, they found out that he had been lying to them about his health; their dad was still under a doctor's care. Her dad had no business being on a slide. His girlfriend had begged him not to get on the slide, but he was determined to make the day memorable for Gracie. He told her that he wasn't sure how much time he had left and wanted to do this with his baby girl. Suddenly it all made sense that he would plan a family beach trip after all these years apart. The heart attack scared him.

CHAPTER 13

Time to Follow Adonai's Plan Now

It had been ten long months since the beach trip. Gracie and her dad talked on the phone almost every day since; Gracie had to make sure he was okay. She had become very protective of him. That day saving his life changed hers forever; it uniquely bonded them.

This birthday was going to be the best one ever. Gracie would get to spend it with her dad for the first time since he left so many years ago. Things were turning around in their relationship, and she was so thankful for this opportunity to get to know him as his adult daughter.

On Friday, they made plans for connecting on Monday after she got off work, and they would have dinner together. She could hardly wait. Monday had finally arrived; it seemed like the weekend lasted forever. She had to go to work and could hardly wait for the workday to be over so she could see him. Gracie was eating lunch at her desk so that she could leave early to meet him. Suddenly her husband showed up at her desk.

"What are you doing here? What's wrong?" she asked.

He responded, "Gracie, your grandmother called. Your dad's body was discovered this morning in his apartment. The coroner believes he died of a heart attack in his apartment on Friday night."

Gracie gasped. Her head was reeling. She had no response. Her mind was racing, replaying their last phone conversation in her head. She had just talked to him on Friday morning, making plans for the week. This can't be possible. He seemed fine when they spoke.

Gracie sat there stunned. She was speechless and didn't know what to say. Gracie was too stunned to cry, yet, she thought back to all their conversations, their vacation the previous summer. It was her birthday week. He was supposed to spend it with her. This was not the plan! How could this be happening? Then the thought suddenly hit Gracie; her dad had abandoned her again. This time, it was permanent. As that realization sunk in, the tears began to flow down her face slowly.

Her dad was found dead on the kitchen floor of his condo mid-morning Monday, April 10. According to the emergency responders, he had fixed an Alka-Seltzer, apparently thinking he had indigestion, but died before he had a chance to drink it.

He had last talked to Gracie Friday morning, confirming their plans for Monday night. He had talked to his girlfriend later that day on the phone, and she didn't expect to hear from him again until he got back from Birmingham the following week. His mom was expecting to hear from him Monday morning before he left Destin. So no one was looking for him all weekend.

When her grandmother had not heard from him Monday morning, she began to worry. She called the superintendent of his condo and had them go check on him. They found his body and immediately called 911.

Due to him being dead for three days in the floor, it was not possible for an open casket. Thereby dashing all hopes of any closure. Without seeing his body, Gracie could imagine he just ran away from everyone. She allowed herself to wonder if he was on a deserted island with Elvis hiding out. Meaning that back then, there were so many rumors that Elvis wasn't dead but hiding out on a deserted island. Gracie needed to imagine that her dad was on that island, still alive too. Not forever, just long enough for her twenty-two-year-old brain to wrap her head around his passing and her loss and abandonment from the man that meant the most in the world to her. The man she so wanted to love her and be there for her but never was able to make that happen. She believed he loved her; he just couldn't get past all his demons in his head to be a dad. He used to tell she and her brother all the time that he would never live to be fifty. Gracie hated it when he said that and wondered how he knew that. Her dad was gone from a massive heart attack at age forty-seven.

Gracie reflected on how she had not been able to spend enough time with him. He was supposed to live to be an old grandpa and always be there when she needed to call him, to watch his grandkids grow up, to have long talks about life and lessons learned. Gracie was devastated never to see him again. She didn't get to say goodbye; she didn't get closure.

Six months later, her aunt Molly, who was like a mother to her, died from a brain aneurism. It was a challenging year of loss for Gracie. Gracie's dad's death put further strain on her already troubled marriage. The year following her dad's death was a blur. She kept wanting to call his phone number and have him answer. It had to be a dream. Without seeing his body for herself, she found it so hard to believe that he was gone. It was easier to keep thinking he must have run away or something. How was she to process this level of abandonment from him?

At this point in her life, her reaction would be different this time he left her. She had allowed Adonai to work on her heart over the years. There were still so many feelings to sort through; she still had abandonment issues. As Gracie prayed for Adonai to heal her heart and help her accept his death, she felt Adonai was telling her to give all those feelings to Him to carry (Matthew 11:30). She heard Him say in her heart that her dad couldn't love her like she needed to be loved. That night, Gracie felt that He told her in her heart to name her feelings and box them up in an imaginary box, wrap it with a bow, and give it to Him, let it go and give it to Him with all the feelings inside. The deal was that once she let them go and offered to Him, she couldn't take the feelings back. She trusted Him and did as He instructed. It was such a freeing process as she prayed and did as He said (Luke 1:13). She discovered something amazing in His Word while spending time with Him as He healed her heart: Adonai created us to crave a love that only He can give (Romans 5:5, John 3:16, John 14:23, John 15:9). For years, Gracie searched for love and acceptance from people when no human could fill her with the love that only Adonai could give her. The discovery of the depth of His love was a game-changer for Gracie (Ephesians 3:14–21). Adonai showed her that she had put unreasonable expectations on people to do things that only He could do for her.

Gracie felt so much better about the loss after that night. It was genuinely freeing for her to trust Adonai to carry the burden of her feelings (Mark 15:21). It was also the beginning of something new in her as she allowed herself to trust in His love and let Him love her like she's always needed (1 John 4:16).

Even though Gracie was turning a corner from the loss, she couldn't shake the feeling that she had the flu. She finally went to the doctor to see if something else was going on. The doctor said, "Congratulations! You're pregnant!" Gracie was stunned. Then she cried, realizing that her baby would never know her dad. His first grandchild, Phillip, was born thirteen months after his death.

Six months after Phillip was born, the flu symptoms returned. Surprise! Gracie was pregnant again. She couldn't stop crying. Having a child did not help her already struggling marriage, as she had hoped. Having the responsibility of a second child in a troubled marriage overwhelmed Gracie. She prayed and told Adonai the only way she could be happy about being pregnant again at this point in her life was if He gave her a girl. She had always prayed for Adonai to give her a daughter that she could be best friends. Her prayers were answered (Luke 1:13). He blessed her with sweet baby Caroline.

Gracie had no interest in being divorced ever, especially once she had two babies. Her dream was to marry a man madly in love with her, and they would grow old together. Maybe that would have happened if she had allowed Adonai to direct her path instead of telling Him what course she was taking. Sadly, it seemed that no matter how she tried to fix things with her husband, they couldn't get past their problems. In her view, their marriage was void of love or happiness; they fought constantly. Her inability to deal with the loss of her dad was a massive barrier in her marriage, along with her abandonment issues. Combined, the problems they faced could not prevent the imminent demise of their fifteen-year marriage.

CHAPTER 14

Time to Go

Gracie and her husband were both miserable with their mountain of problems. Her husband blamed her for their problems, and rightly so; even still, he didn't want to divorce. Gracie couldn't continue to live like that; she felt like he was punishing her for all her mistakes. She didn't need his help punishing her; she was doing plenty of that on her own. Someone had to make the decision to "stop the bleeding" (Genesis 13:8–9). It was not healthy for any of them to stay together. Then, when Gracie thought all hope was lost and became desperate for direction, she cried out to God and told Him she couldn't do it anymore. She said, "I repent, Father. Please forgive me for telling you what to do and trying to control my life. Please forgive me for ignoring the signs you tried to show me. I now give my life to you. Please help us. Please show me what to do." Then Adonai answered her prayers. He said, "Gracie, it's time to move your tent. We are moving it to the land of hope." He said, "If you will trust me and move your tent, I will bless you" (Genesis 13:18, Acts 2:26).

Gracie was scared but clung to His hand, held her breath, and clenched her eyes shut as she stepped out in faith (Matthew 14:29). When she took the kids and left for their protection and sanity, her husband used the fatal word. He told everyone that Gracie had "abandoned him and had taken the kids." How ironic that she was being accused of the very thing that she had run from her entire life. Anyone knowing the scars that abandonment does to a person would know that someone running from it would never do it to someone else without reasonable cause. A person fighting abandonment doesn't want to be alone, ever. In fact, that's the last thing they want; they think they need people. When a scarred person who battles being abandoned leaves a relationship, it's for their health and survival. They are not trying to hurt the person they left, they are trying to find personal healing.

Gracie didn't expect he or his family to understand but prayed that one day they would find it in their hearts to forgive her for leaving her marriage and leaving them. She prayed her kids would forgive her and one day understand why she had to break up their family. It was the hardest thing she ever did, but Adonai said, "It's time to go. It's time to follow me now." After the years she spent in that toxic relationship, Gracie left with no self-esteem or self-confidence. When she left for good, all she could do was cry. She felt like such a failure. Suddenly Gracie found herself in similar shoes that her mom was in so many years before, raising two kids on her own. The kids were seven and eight when they split. Her husband wouldn't leave their house, so they were forced to move in with her mom in her tiny garden home. She was so thankful that her mom didn't say "I told you so" but opened her home and disrupted her life without hesitation to take them in. Fortunately, her mom was able to help her take care of the kids. Gracie would work all day and then come home and cry herself to sleep most nights. Trusting God doesn't mean the road will be easy.

Through the two-year divorce process, she found out who her real friends were. All of her current church friends told her she was going to hell for leaving him. The rest of her friends heard his version of the story first, that she abandoned him and took the kids; she assumed they believed him, and they suddenly disappeared. Gracie did not have the energy to go behind him and try to explain herself to everyone; she had to resolve to let whoever say whatever. She had to trust Adonai to take care of her and all the details. He told her, "Trust me. You don't have to justify your actions. You need to focus on obeying Me and following Me." So she did what she learned years before, trust and pray (Mark 15:1–5). Gracie followed Adonai's example and didn't say anything. She prayed that Adonai would carry her through yet another battle in her life. Gracie was counting on Him to do what He had always done. She trusted Him completely. At her lowest, Gracie gave Him all she had (Mark 14:4). Gracie was scared to take that first step to leave; it was a huge step that she never thought she would need to take. She put all her trust in Adonai and stepped out clenching His hand walking in blind faith (Luke 1:28, 30). He spoke to her heart and said, "Don't be afraid, I Am your protector" (Genesis 15:1). He said, "Gracie, I am with you always" (Matthew 28:20).

Gracie learned the hard way that apart from Adonai, we can do nothing (John 15:5). Throughout her marriage to Jimmy, she prayed that Adonai would forgive her for disobeying Him and telling Him whom she would marry (Revelations 3:19). She knew that He heard her prayers and forgave her, but she also knew what His Word says, "We reap what we sow" (Galatians 6:7). She knew that her decisions came with consequences; she had to pay for her sins. She tried to make the best of the situation and not complain to Adonai (Mark 8:34). When things never got better but got worse over time, she prayed eventually for a way out; she even offered up her life to get out. She was that miserable (1 Corinthians 10:13). She couldn't bear the thought of leaving her kids, but she couldn't take the fighting and verbal abuse anymore.

She knew something had to change when her son began to talk to her like his dad was doing. Phillip was such a good boy; she didn't want her kids to suffer the effects of growing up in that negative environment. Caroline and her dad fought almost as much as he did with Gracie. She knew that after fifteen years of fighting with no improvement that the situation wasn't going to change, they had no choice but to go for the betterment of all. The definition of insanity is doing the same thing over and over, expecting different results. It was time for the insanity to stop, time to get away from the problem again. Gracie had spent so many years trying to force happiness into her marriage, like forcing a square peg into a round hole. It was never going to work. It would be many years before Gracie learned that her husband wasn't her problem; she was her problem. She needed healing.

Gracie knew what Adonai's Word says about divorce; she did not want to do something He highly disapproved. She had made so many bad decisions over the years, but she knew Adonai still loved her and forgave her when she repented (Acts 3:19). Gracie was always one to learn from her mistakes. She didn't need to be punished because she punished herself plenty. Gracie didn't like to disappoint the Father; when she did, she promised Adonai never to do it again, and she didn't. Gracie still made mistakes but generally not the same ones; she meant it when she repented.

In this extremely difficult situation, Gracie prayed for guidance, wisdom, and discernment. She wanted to do things Adonai's way this time (Deuteronomy 26:17). There was no way she would leave unless He opened doors for her to go and provided what she needed to get through the process. She knew ending her life wasn't His answer, and if He didn't open doors for her to leave, she told Him that she would stay as long as He stayed and protected her and the kids. She said to Him that she was putting all her trust in Him. Gracie knew she could trust her heavenly Father; she knew He would go before her and make a way when there seemed to be no way (Deuteronomy 10:12).

Adonai heard her prayers (Luke 1:13). To her surprise, He began opening doors (Deuteronomy 30:16). In her prayers, crying out for wisdom and direction, He said, "Follow me. Don't be afraid; just keep trusting" (Mark 5:36, Deuteronomy 31:8). She was scared to death. When someone has been in a relationship like theirs for so long, it was tough to leave. With no self-confidence and no self-esteem at this point, it was a debilitating thought for her to go. She feared her husband's temper. When her heavenly Father said, "Follow me. Don't be afraid, just keep trusting" (Mark 5:36), she knew from experience that He would take care of her and the kids. Her heavenly Father said, "Let's go. I will go with you and give you rest." Gracie said, "If you don't go with us, please just leave us here." He grabbed her hand and said, "Fear not, for I am with you." Gracie clung to His hand as He led them out (John 16:32, Isaiah 41:13). Even though it was a traumatic exit for all of them, she prayed constantly and clung to His promises as she weathered the storms with her heavenly Father leading the way.

Gracie later labeled these scary, audacious moments Adonai walked her through as "out of the boat" moments. When He called her out of the boat like He did Peter in the Bible story, she would take a deep breath and follow, clinging to His hand every step (Matthew 14:29). As she walked through the steps of the divorce, she received help from the most unlikely people. When each person He sent to help her was done with their part in the process, suddenly another person would pop up to help her get through the next step. The divorce process and the tactics from her husband and his attorney created incredible stress for her; including, but not limited, to her husband handing over all her journals and Bible study notebooks to his attorney. All her deepest thoughts were in front of the opposing attorney and later read in court. To say that experience was unthinkably horrible doesn't accurately describe how she felt. She spent the entire two years crying over the constant character attacks against her but she knew that Adonai was walking every step with her holding her. When church people judged her, she withdrew from them. Gracie didn't have to justify herself; Adonai was in control (Isaiah 53:7). He told her to trust Him, and she did (Romans 8:6). This was her first big test at totally trusting Him, and she was determined to pass. She decided she was tired of trying to control her life; it was exhausting. She was ready to follow her heavenly Father and let Him lead her on the path He had for her (Psalm 119:35, 105; Proverbs 12:28). It wasn't an easy path, but it was already proving to be a more peaceful path with Him at her side (Job 28:7, Psalm 16:11, Proverbs 15:24).

After the divorce was final, some lifelong friends who had stopped talking to Gracie were suddenly calling again. Old friends were speaking out, letting her know that they knew him and they knew her. They didn't believe a word he said but didn't want to get involved in the divorce. They were calling to check on her to make sure she knew that they still believed in her. Gracie cried at the revelation. After two long years and a week in court on trial, it was finally over. The divorce was final; she and the kids could get on with their lives.

Gracie witnessed how her heavenly Father walked out every step of her life to this point. Anyone who believes, like Gracie, that Adonai doesn't like divorce will hopefully see that there are cases where He will rescue His children from unacceptable circumstances regardless of how they came about. It's important to have repentant hearts seeking to be obedient and trust Him when we make mistakes.

CHAPTER 15

Adonai, What's Next?

Who was Gracie now? What was next for her and the kids? She was exhausted from all the tricks the opposing attorney used on her to draw things out and run up the legal bills. Gracie had cried for so many years that she was numb and depleted, void of self-confidence and self-esteem. She wondered how to move forward. All her perfect life plans were crushed; another chapter closed. Gracie realized she had no plan or direction. She felt like a failure, wondering how she got to that point. She never dreamed she would be a single divorced mother; that was never in her dreams. What she did know to be the truth is that Adonai led them out, and He had a plan for her that she couldn't see; she just had to keep following Him, not be afraid and keep trusting Him (Mark 5:32, 36).

One of the many painful tricks used on Gracie during the divorce to get full custody of her kids was to prove she was having an affair with someone. Much to her horror, there was a list of men from work who suddenly received a subpoena. Then her husband and his attorney attempted to see if they could prove she was having an affair with any of them. Gracie was mortified; no one at work knew she was going through a divorce. Suddenly the secret was out.

As the legal bills piled up, all their tricks failed to prove Gracie was having an affair or was an unfit mother. Their best efforts failed, but as her heavenly Father always does, He brings something good out of something terrible (Romans 8:38). As a result of the spontaneous subpoenas, Gracie met her soul mate. What was meant to devastate and destroy Gracie, Adonai used the opportunity to turn the horrible action into a positive outcome for Gracie. The least likely person to ever catch Gracie's eye romantically was the one her heavenly Father chose for her.

In the latter years of her failing marriage, Gracie imagined what qualities the perfect spouse would possess if Adonai ever gave her another chance. She remembered back to what the pastor had said all those many years ago in the church group after high school. Having realized after the fact that he meant for them to name the qualities, not the name of a person, she began to dream about the qualities her true love would have in her imaginary perfect world.

Gracie never put those thoughts on paper; she learned the hard way what happens when you put things in print. She was horrified when she found out that her ex-husband had taken all of her diaries and Bible study journals and had given them to his attorney to use against her in court. Fortunately, she had the foresight not to make a written wish list of the perfect spouse. The only one that knew about this "perfect spouse" list was her and her heavenly Father, the One in her life that she could truly trust. Adonai helped her make the mental list years ago, but she had no way of knowing that He already had a plan and someone created just for her, in His perfect timing.

During her marriage, Gracie had worked at a corporation for over ten years and loved her job. Her first job there required her to interact with employees all over the building. There was a manager in the building named Wally that she had known of for a long time. He had worked there many years before she was hired. Their paths crossed sporadically throughout her employment with over five thousand employees in the large high-rise building. The first time she met him, she was interviewing for an admin job in his department that was given to someone else.

Some six years after that interview, Gracie found herself caught up in a corporate organizational structure change. Her new assignment would be working directly for Wally as his Administrative Assistant. At that time in his life, he was super intense and under a lot of pressure in his job, which made for a very unpleasant work environment. She worked for him about six months when upper management moved her again to another department. Gracie was relieved when they moved her away from him. Working for him was affecting her health negatively; she developed hives during that time that went away not long after she was out from under that stressful environment.

The change in jobs was good for Gracie. She thrived in each area she worked; no one ever had a clue she was unhappily married. Being at work helped distract her from the problems at home; it was good for her to have that break during the day. Until she had said "I do," she would have removed herself from a problem if there was no hope of rectifying it. This time, it was different. Marriage is a commitment for life that she did not take lightly. She thought that Adonai would bless it because it was what she "wanted." More importantly, she was determined not to let her mom be right about him not being the one for her. Somehow she had to make it work.

It had been a couple of years since Gracie had moved from working from Wally. She was rocking along, enjoying her job, when another reorganization popped up. Suddenly and without warning, Wally moved into her department as one of the managers Gracie supported. Gracie was stronger now and felt she was more prepared to deal with his intense personality but at the same time was not looking forward to more hives.

Not long after his move, she discovered he was a very different man. He was still a type A personality, very driven, but he was calmer. She heard that the job he moved from had taken a toll on him even though he was successful at reaching his intended goal and that he had also gone through a tough divorce. The Wally that Gracie met as one of her new bosses was not the same man she had worked for years before.

CHAPTER 16

The Secret Was Out

Despite her problems at home, Gracie always tried to spread joy wherever she was; she had the gift of encouragement. She felt that was her calling from her heavenly Father, to spread His love with others; this was her focus when away from home, not talking about her problems to others. Gracie was a hard worker, and management had come to depend on her whenever they needed something done and done right; she had earned respect among her peers and management.

When her husband's attorney pulled out her latest trick, sending subpoenas to her coworkers, it came as a complete surprise to Gracie. The day that Wally and others received a subpoena in her divorce sent her reeling with embarrassment and concern for her job. Being a private person, this invasion of her privacy brought on by her soon-to-be ex-husband was crushing to her already fragile spirit in her failing marriage. How was she going to recover from this at work? Everyone thought she was happy; she was always happy. One of the expectations from her coworkers and management was that Gracie was always joyful. How could she be joyful when her marriage was falling apart? Only by the grace of Adonai (John 1:16, Acts 4:33).

Gracie had no idea about the subpoenas until Wally called her in his office one day and said in a stern tone, "What is this?" while holding a folded piece of paper. She looked at him, confused. She took the piece of paper, and as she read it, her heart sank. The paper slid out of her hand onto the floor as tears began to stream down her face. It took every ounce of strength she had to look up at his wondering eyes and admit that she was getting divorced.

There! She had said it out loud. She was getting divorced. The secret was out. Up until that point, no one knew but her family. The announcement made it seem more real somehow. In a matter of days, word would spread around the entire building that Gracie was unhappy at home.

Gracie was so embarrassed and tried to compose herself as she explained the situation to Wally. She told him she was in the fight of her life to keep her kids. It was not in Wally's plan to get involved; he had been blindsided by this document. He had issues of his own to work through. After his bitter divorce, he had sworn off women, assuming that they were all out to break a man's heart. However, after hearing her story, he felt compelled to help. It was as if an inner force outside of his control made him say, "I want to help you keep your kids." Gracie sat in a daze as she was still trying to process the evilness of the opposing attorney's latest attack on her character. Lost in her thoughts, when he offered to help, all she could hear were muffled words that sounded far away.

Wally realized that her lack of reaction indicated that she hadn't heard him. He repeated his offer. Gracie slowly returned to reality as Wally asked the second time if she would allow him to help. She wondered to herself, *Why would he want to help me? He doesn't even know me.* He had no obligation to help her. She heard herself ask him, "Why? Why would you do that?" While Wally listened to her story, he was surprised to hear that Gracie's opposing attorney was the exact attorney his ex used against him. He said, "I want to help you for several reasons." Two reasons on the list of many were (1) he didn't want her to lose her kids and (2) he had more motivation due to the opportunity to be on the offense with the opposing attorney who had previously put him through hell on earth. He thought it surely must be fate that he got this opportunity, an opportunity to right some wrongs for both of them. He had nothing but time on his hands; his kids were grown and had lives of their own. Gracie was stunned when he said that he wanted to help. Numb from the latest news from the attorney, she accepted his offer.

Adonai used the painful embarrassing circumstance of the subpoena to bring Wally in Gracie's life, and He used him to step up to help Gracie win her case. He gave her input and advice on how to get through the process and keep her kids. Gracie will forever remember how horrifying it was to have coworkers forced on the stand to testify to her character while also having to watch them have to endure an unbearable drilling of accusations for them to refute that they were not having an affair with her. It was all horrifying but not as painful as watching her children have to be put on the stand and questioned about what kind of mother she was to them. It is forever etched in her mind when she had to watch a former female coworker, who always hated Gracie's positive attitude, get up on the stand and lie about her character. It was then, with her hand over her mouth to keep from blurting out from the lies she was subjected to listen to under oath, that Gracie, in horror under her breath, asked Adonai, "Am I going to lose my kids over these lies?" In that moment, Adonai immediately gave her three questions to have her attorney ask the woman to prove she was lying. Gracie quickly leaned over and told him to ask her those three questions. Her attorney asked the questions, and the witness was instantly exposed as not telling the truth, and it was clear to the judge that she was lying.

The judge dismissed her and told the opposing attorney, "This dog and pony show has gone on long enough. Closing remarks are tomorrow."

The attorney immediately panicked and jumped up, spouting nervously, "I haven't been able to bring in all the people I have subpoenaed yet!"

The judge responded, "Closing remarks tomorrow!"

Gracie sat there stunned at what had happened. The three questions worked. As easily as the questions were given to her from Adonai, they were gone. She has never been able to remember what they were. It doesn't really matter. Adonai took care of her as always.

The next day, the judge ruled in her favor! He awarded Gracie full custody, mandatory child support, and a list of other things, including assigning all legal fees for both of them to her brand-new ex-husband. Adonai gave her favor (Luke 1:28). He was with her every step, every minute. In court for a week and on the stand for two days, being grilled by the opposing attorney was the scariest experience ever for Gracie. She prayed through the entire week. Gracie didn't have the strength to get through the hell of the court process alone; she had to cling to Adonai and rely on His strength for survival. Her heavenly Father promised her He would bless her if she trusted Him and remained steadfast under trial (James 1:12).

Gracie held Adonai's hand and trusted Him. She followed Him, and He led her and the kids out (Genesis 15:7, Luke 1:28). Nothing is impossible with Adonai (Luke 1:37). Gracie trusted Him; He blessed her because she trusted her heavenly Father, and He fulfilled His promises to her. No matter what we are going through, no matter how horrible, we can get through it with unexplainable peace if we will put ourselves and our circumstances in Adonai's hands.

An unexpected blessing in the whole ordeal, a year into her divorce, Wally was forced into her personal life by a subpoena. As a result of that subpoena, she found her soul mate that she had prayed for her entire life. Adonai had finally brought him to her. Adonai's timing is perfect, and their time to be together had finally arrived.

CHAPTER 17

Gift from the Father

During the divorce process, Gracie got to know Wally on a personal level. It was at that time that Gracie made a fantastic discovery. She recalled her mental checklist that she had worked on so many years before, the list of what the perfect man for her would look like if He gave her another chance. Unaware of this secret list, Wally unknowingly checked all the boxes.

Once the divorce was over, Wally had done his job. He fully expected Gracie to move on with her new life, and he prepared to do the same; he helped get justice for them both. He was glad that the outcome was favorable for her and the kids.

Of all the valuable lessons Gracie had learned over the years, one of the most important was to listen to her heavenly Father, to trust Him with every detail of her life and not to tell Him what to do. She had learned that He knows best; He has a perfect plan for her and doesn't need her advice (Jeremiah 29:11). Gracie made countless mistakes and relationship failures. She was looking to Adonai now for guidance for what was next (Matthew 6:24). All of us have options: do things His way or do them our way. Humbled by Adonai, Gracie wanted to stay there, close to Adonai, where it was peaceful. He gives grace to the humble (Luke 8:48, James 4:6).

If Wally was truly the one, things were going to be different this time. She prayed and prayed to Adonai, "If this is for real and he is the one you created for me, please let me know. I'm waiting on you. I'm not making a move without you. I will not make the same mistake twice, telling you what to do with my love life."

Today was the day. Gracie found a large brown envelope in the mailbox from her attorney. She quickly opened it and was so relieved to find the official divorce papers signed off by the judge. It was finally over! Tears flowed down her cheeks as she thanked Adonai for all He had done for her. Regardless of the consequences she suffered and the pain of the process, she was grateful for all Adonai had done. After all the help Wally had given her, she couldn't wait to get on the phone and let him know it was over. He was excited for her and was grateful that he was able to help do some good. They decided it was a call for celebration. That night, they went to dinner to celebrate the victory and her newfound freedom for her and the kids. Over dinner, they discussed the painful events in her life the last two years and how interesting it was how Adonai brought them together in such a unique way. Gracie decided to tell him about her mental checklist of the perfect husband for her. Wally found humor listening to her telling the story. What he didn't expect was for her to say that he had checked all the boxes. She said, "I believe Adonai created us for each other. You are the man I've prayed for all my life. I just didn't know it was you until now." Wally sat stunned and speechless. After all they had been through, he couldn't help but care for Gracie and her children, but he had zero expectations for anything between them. After Wally's past relationship issues with women in his life, he wasn't ready to give his heart to another. He had trust issues and was expecting Gracie to move on after her divorce was final. His hesitation didn't bother Gracie. She was at peace with his fears and concerns. She knew that it would all work out if it was meant to be; she was trusting Adonai this time. Gracie suggested that they focus on getting to know each other as friends. They enjoyed each other's company, so why not continue being friends? He agreed.

Wally spent the following two years in an internal battle all of his own. His heart was betraying him, and his affection for her continued to grow. Every time he wanted to tell her he loved her, he would push her away to protect his heart. He didn't trust his heart to stick to the plan. He tried to, at the very least, attempt to keep her at arm's length. His efforts failed; he couldn't stay away from her. Gracie played it cool, trusting and praying as Adonai tested her to see if she was going to let Him maintain control of her life. Then suddenly, one day, Wally surprised her and said, "Want to get married next month?" Without hesitation, Gracie gleefully said yes! The last two years turned out to be the biggest test of patience for Gracie; she assumed she passed when Wally finally proposed. For Wally, that time was vital to him to make sure this was for real and that Gracie wasn't just rebounding. She also wanted to make sure that it was Adonai's plan. Gracie didn't want another marriage for the sake of being married. She wanted to marry her soulmate and be happy. She knew if Adonai blessed this union, everything would be okay. If only everything could be so simple. Not surprisingly, her mom did not approve of that marriage news either. It would be years after their marriage before she came around and realized that Wally was the perfect one for Gracie, at least she came around though.

After spending lots of time together those two years prior to the proposal, Gracie and the kids were all on the same page. Wally told her that Adonai came to him in a dream, Adonai asked him how much more proof and time did he need to realize that she was the one He sent to Wally. When Adonai said it was right, he knew it was safe for him to commit and give his heart to Gracie.

After weeks of pre-marriage counseling and getting wedding details the way they wanted, they tied the knot with their combined four kids standing by their sides. Neither could stop smiling. Their marriage was a gift from Adonai that neither expected nor thought they deserved; they were so grateful for repentance, grace, and forgiveness from the heavenly Father above (Mark 16:7). They laughed together as they remembered back to when she worked for him. Gracie had just married the man who years ago gave her hives.

Twenty years his junior, neither of them noticed the age difference. They were so in love that nothing mattered. Each of them was determined to follow Adonai in this marriage and get it right this time. Together they decided to keep Him at the center of their marriage no matter what came their way, and both agreed that there was no back door to their marriage. They were in it for life, for better or for worse, in sickness and in health, until death parts them.

No marriage is perfect, but Gracie and Wally were dedicated to Adonai and to each other to be a team through whatever came their way.

CHAPTER 18

A New Chapter for All

It proved to be quite challenging adjusting to living together for the four of them, but they made it work. It had been a long time since Wally had lived with young kids in the house. Phillip and Caroline were eleven and twelve at that time; pre-teen hormones are an adjustment all on their own without adding on a new home life and family. Gracie and Wally got into a rhythm in their new life together, then suddenly found themselves dealing with health issues, unexpected challenges hitting them right away. He was a very loving and attentive caregiver for Gracie when needed. Wally had lovingly nursed her through a hysterectomy caused by endometriosis. Then Gracie got the opportunity to nurse him through double knee replacement surgery that Wally was determined to have done on the same day so that it would be over. He could not walk for six weeks, so Gracie did everything for him with extreme unforeseen complications. That was quite a challenge for 5 ft. nothing 120 lbs. to do everything by herself for 6'3", 220. It was by the grace of Adonai and her sheer determination to take care of her beloved that got them through recovery until he was on his feet again. After riding that crazy storm of recovery together, Wally had no question how much Gracie loved him. They went through things in his recovery that most newlyweds would never survive. Gracie cared for him without hesitation, doing whatever he needed; it was her nature. She loved taking care of her husband. They were a team.

Having survived the trauma of his double knee surgery and getting him back to his daily routine, they were glad to have a break from surgery and nursing duties without knee pain. Before they knew it, their love was being tested again. They barely caught their breath from his recovery and were hit again. Gracie received the devastating news that she had the markers for breast cancer at the same age her mother developed breast cancer. They prayed about it, talked to several specialists, and decided to be proactive and allow the doctors to perform a double radical mastectomy.

Wally's turn to step back up and nurse Gracie again arose quickly. Together, along with their faith and trust in Adonai, they were going headfirst into a long journey with surgery and recovery process. He didn't complain about changing her drains four times a day, getting her meds, bathing her, feeding her, and whatever else she needed. He just wanted her well. He wanted his Gracie back. He couldn't bear the thought of losing her. Wally did his best to dry and style her hair; Gracie had to quickly draw the line at that task. That sweet man tried so hard; with his best efforts, her hair looked horrible. He would try blowing it dry with no brush; he couldn't figure out how to use the brush through her hair. When Wally finished drying her hair, she looked like Gilda Radner from Saturday Night Live. At a time when there wasn't much to laugh about, they both got tickled at the outcome of her hair. He suggested she call her hairdresser. Gracie was blessed to have a hairdresser at the time that volunteered to go to her house a few times a week to wash and style her hair.

They were both trying to work full-time jobs after her initial six-week recovery period. The process was such a challenge, but they made it work. The surgery recoveries each time just bonded them closer together.

Even though they were so close, so happy, and had survived so much together, Gracie secretly still battled her abandonment issues. Gracie thought he was the most beautiful man in the world. No matter where they went, women were always flirting with him. He wouldn't flirt with them, but he would be kind. His kindness always seemed to encourage the women to keep flirting. With her chest totally removed from surgery, she "assumed" the threat of him leaving her for a beautiful woman was even higher. It was hard on Gracie; the enemy was constantly spewing lies in her mind that Wally would leave her for someone else. It didn't matter how much he assured her that he loved and adored her. Based on her experience with her mom and dad, she believed that the "right" woman with the "right words" and the "right clothes and seduction plan" could steal him away in a heartbeat.

Wally had to travel often on business. When he would leave town, Gracie would go into a funk until he got back home. He called her all the time and talked about how much he missed her and loved her. Gracie just couldn't shake the feeling that one day she was going to get a call like her mom had gotten from her dad and like she had received from Beau.

What Gracie didn't understand at the time was how loyal Wally was. She didn't understand or know his past well enough to know that he adored her and would never leave her as long as she adored him and loved him too. He wanted their marriage to work as much as Gracie did. She knew her heart and commitment to the relationship but couldn't see his total commitment; blinded to the truth about his love for her, all she could hear were the enemies' lies in her head. Fears of him finding someone better consumed Gracie. She was always waiting for the dreaded phone call.

Gracie wasted so many years waiting for that call. They had great times when they were together; they traveled and did so many fun things too. He always made her smile, and they laughed at the silliest things. Wally constantly did something that a loyal husband would do, but all of her hopes would be momentarily dashed in one flirtatious encounter by a home-wrecker until she could catch her breath long enough for Adonai to show her the truth—how much Wally loved her.

Since the day Wally was thrust into her life, Wally encouraged Gracie throughout their time together. He worked tirelessly building up her self-confidence and self-esteem. Wally helped her in many ways; he was so good for her. With all his best efforts, she just couldn't shake her fears of him abandoning her; what she didn't know until years later, he was always concerned that she would grow tired of him and leave. They were both so deeply in love with each other but had unintentionally allowed the enemy to creep in with fears of losing what Adonai had given them. Despite their fears, Adonai protected their relationship and led them toward finding the truth. Adonai had big plans to heal them both, but Gracie still had to hit bottom first so Adonai could prune and refine her to get her where He needed to her be in order for her healing to begin.

CHAPTER 19

Where Did Hope Go?

How did she get to this place? Why did it seem like her world was coming to an end? Where had her faith gone? Why couldn't she function normally? Wasn't there anything that she could control anymore? Everything seemed to change after her double radical mastectomy. Having her chest removed was drastic and immediate, it all happened so fast. Now her struggles had reached a severe level as gradually everything in her world seemed to spiral out of control. At the time, there was no way to know what was real. Was she losing her mind, or was it all the meds she had ingested from all the surgery procedures with her double radical mastectomy? So much anesthesia and so many meds to do this and that, her body couldn't take it anymore. Gracie had so many internal battles going on at this time and couldn't reason things out logically; it was the perfect internal storm. She was so blessed and so loved, yet her fears were trying to consume her. How could this be? She had always possessed great faith and totally trusted Adonai; He never left her even when she made mistakes. Gracie knew not to carry her fears, not to let them pitch a tent and move in; she always gave them to Adonai. Why was that process not working now? Gracie mentally battled her thoughts on self-worth and prayed to Adonai asking, "What is wrong with me? Why am I carrying this battle, Father? Why aren't you carrying it for me? Please help me." This went on for months with no relief.

She worked hard to put on a front pretending she was okay, but it proved difficult. Her mind couldn't convince her body to snap out of it, whatever it was. She had convinced herself that hiding her pain was the best idea/lie.

Even though she had a husband that adored her and couldn't breathe without her love, Gracie was extremely uncomfortable and insecure about her current state of disfigurement. She had been fighting self-esteem issues since the surgery and trying to grasp how deformed her body looked before the rebuilding process could begin; it really messed with her head. She couldn't remember feeling so ugly; she couldn't even look at herself in the mirror. She constantly thought to herself, *How can Wally bare to look at me?*

Gracie had always been a very positive person, a person that others looked to for encouragement and inspiration. To know her was to know that she never complained and always looked for the positives in the negatives so much so that sometimes it would annoy others when they were down and didn't want encouragement. There was one time when she was trying to encourage a girl that told her that she wished she would just be mad with her and not try to cheer her up. That was the first time Gracie realized that there is a time for encouragement and a time for listening. Everyone always knew that if they saw Gracie, they were to expect a hug. Gracie couldn't bear the thought of someone not having at least one hug a day. When they came to church, it was her mission as a greeter to make sure that everyone had at least one hug for the day. She loves making people feel special and known (1 Corinthians 8:3). When she was growing up it crushed her when she saw people who were left out in a crowd. She has always gone out of her way to make everyone feel special and included.

Having the gift of encouragement is such a blessing, but there is a downside as well. The downside is that everyone expects you to be upbeat all the time, always encouraging. Just like with anyone else, there are times when an encourager is down and needs to lean on someone for encouragement. When this happens, it's like others suddenly don't know how to communicate with them, thereby causing an encourager to withdraw. People don't realize it, but they become so dependent on encouragers that they don't know how to act when an encourager needs encouraging. The upside to an encourager withdrawing is that they lean on the only one they can truly trust, Adonai, our God. He is the only one who understands and the only one who can help and heal all of us.

Gracie wanted so badly to have a person to talk to about what she was going through but didn't know how to make that happen because she didn't know for sure what was wrong with her. She was afraid to let Wally and Caroline know she was struggling, which didn't make sense. She always went to them for advice and input. Instead, she did the best she could to hide her pain and struggles.

On this particular day, all of her fears and worries that she couldn't shake and had been battling alone were getting the best of her. Gracie had reached the depths of despair, somewhere she had never been before. She thought to herself, *So this is what it feels like to want to end your life?* She had never understood suicide and had always feared Adonai too much to consider taking her life into her own hands. This is when she realized that her state of mind was not right for her to even consider it. She had always believed that Adonai uses every circumstance in our lives (Romans 8:28). Gracie always believed that she couldn't help others with something if she had no firsthand knowledge of the problem herself. At the time, she did not have the clarity of mind to realize that Adonai was going to use this trial for His glory to help others through her. She had always prayed for Adonai to use her whenever, however, whatever. What good is an encourager if they have no life experience to help others? It's not a requirement to have the gift of encouragement to help others. Adonai will use you and your experiences to help others no matter your spiritual gifts, if you let Him.

Wally was headed out of town on business on Monday, which meant she would be in a funk over his absence until he returned later that week. Just as well, she thought he was probably tired of her anyway, post-surgery. Caroline was asleep across the hall from her and had no idea what she was going through. She had been out all day working and then with her boyfriend and didn't get in till late. Phillip no longer lived in the state due to his Army responsibilities.

Gracie was already in bed and had sent a text to Wally and the two youngest kids earlier, randomly telling them that she wanted them to know how much she loved them. She had made the emotional decision to end her life that night and not tell them. In her mind, they would be just fine without her. That is such a lie that the enemy tells someone, and when you are emotionally imbalanced for whatever reason, it's amazing how easy it is to believe that lie from the enemy.

Due to Wally's sleep issues and Gracie's surgery healing issues, Gracie was in the spare room upstairs alone so it made it very easy to make this plan work for her. Her husband had been in the military and had been a weapons instructor and had taught Gracie how to shoot a pistol for protection. Even though they had an alarm system in the home, he kept pistols in each nightstand and various other places you might need protection from an intruder. His home had been invaded many years before Gracie came into his life, so he had always been prepared since then. His perfect planning would have a pistol handy in her nightstand for her to carry out this horrible plan.

She lay crying in bed uncontrollably for hours, thinking about how much she loved Wally and the kids and how she hated for things to end this way. She just couldn't take the pain any longer. Gracie couldn't breathe.

Gracie had prayed her entire life for Wally to come into her life. She just didn't know it was him until Adonai plopped him in her life. She went through so much in her life before Adonai gave him to her. She wished that she could have been perfect for him. Gracie had unintentionally allowed the enemy to convince her that she was too damaged for him to love her. She couldn't see what a lie from the enemy that truly was.

As close as she was to both Wally and Caroline, why wouldn't she confide in them now? Why wouldn't she turn to them so that they could stop her and get her the help she needed? The answer, the weight of the lies from the enemy was so strong that she believed they would be better off without her. She couldn't see truth in this moment. She felt that she had failed as a wife and a parent.

In the depths of despair, she made the only decision she could make. Through swollen blurry eyes from hours of crying, she began to search through the nightstand table to find the pistol. It was no one's fault. Her family loved her, and she loved them. But she believed that she could take the pain no longer. She believed there was only one way to end all her pain in her state of mind. The enemy had her believing that no one would care, that they would go on living their lives just fine without her. She was so distraught that she allowed the enemy's lies to cloud her thinking. Gracie reasoned that Wally could choose from one of the many women who flirted with him. Phillip had moved away and on with his life. She prayed that Adonai would protect Phillip and give him wisdom. Caroline was in love and planning a life with her longtime boyfriend, Jonathan; she prayed and believed that Adonai would protect them. At this point, Gracie believed that no one needed her. She felt like a failure and needed her pain to stop. There was no way for her to know that the meds were helping the enemy play tricks on her mind. The enemy wanted to end her life so that Adonai could not fulfill His purpose in her life.

As Gracie lay there sobbing uncontrollably with the pistol in her hand, she asked, "Adonai, why? Why did You bring me this far to let things end like this?" She knew that Adonai loved her, but at that moment, she couldn't think clearly; she was so far gone that Adonai's love wasn't enough to stop her. She told Adonai she loved Him, but she couldn't take it anymore. She repented because she didn't want to disappoint Adonai. She didn't want to do this horrible thing, but she didn't believe she had a choice. Lying there in bed in the dark bedroom with the TV muted, blinded by her tears, absentmindedly rubbing the trigger in a slow back and forth motion, wondering if she could actually do this, she suddenly saw a vision. It was Caroline. In the vision, Caroline was telling her that she needed her. The vision didn't go away immediately. It lingered long enough for Gracie to understand what was happening. Adonai spoke to Gracie's heart and said, "Stay for her. she needs you." He knew that if any one person could pull her back, it would be Caroline. It worked. He knew that, of course. It wasn't her day to die. Our days are numbered and her number was not up (Psalm 139).

Seeing Caroline's face and hearing those words in her heart and mind snapped Gracie out of her stupor. Adonai had saved her life again; this time, He used Caroline to save her. At the time, Caroline had no idea what Gracie was going through. Days later, after Gracie was feeling a little better, she shared the story with Caroline. She was stunned and horrified but so relieved to hear that Adonai used her to prevent her mom's demise. Caroline and her mom were always very close, but this experience bonded them even closer. When she was at her lowest, Adonai knew Caroline's effect on Gracie's state of mind. When she told Wally what had happened, he was horrified. She assured him that she was okay, that Adonai had stopped her. He hugged her and was afraid to let her go for what seemed like hours. He just cried and prayed and thanked our heavenly Father for saving her life, for saving his Gracie.

There was a good reason for Gracie's behavior that caused this near fatal event, but it wouldn't be until a few days later that she would discover what was wrong with her. She was due for blood work at the doctor. When the results came in, the mystery was solved. As it turned out, Gracie's hormone levels had tanked during her numerous surgeries from her double radical mastectomy. Hormone levels should be in the mid to higher double digits, and Gracie's were in the severely low single digits, literally about to tank. It was no wonder that such a positive, God-fearing woman could entertain the idea of suicide; she couldn't possibly be functioning logically with those numbers. That was great news! The doctors helped get her hormones leveled out, and she was feeling like herself again in no time.

Gracie had often wondered what was in the mind of someone who took their life, especially if they were a person of faith and called themselves a Christian. If you have a relationship with Adonai and read His Word, you will learn that He numbers our days (Psalm 139). It is not okay for us to choose when we go. Gracie had a friend that had a very religious family, and her dad had committed suicide weeks after coming home from the hospital from his open heart surgery. There was no doubt of his faith in Adonai, so it was quite unexpected that he would take his life. As it turned out, the heart meds had a side effect of depression and suicidal thoughts. Gracie had been on so many meds through her surgeries, and with her hormone numbers tanked, it's a miracle that she didn't succumb to the confusion as well.

If you feel like all hope is lost for you, please reach out to someone and get help. There is always hope. Adonai loves you. Call the suicide hotline if you don't have anyone to talk to, but for sure cry out to Adonai. He will send you the help you need. If you are on meds, check the side effects and have a family member aware of what they are as well so that you can avoid this happening to you. Tell those closest to you what you are experiencing. Don't withdraw and listen to the lies. Isolation is the enemy's playground.

CHAPTER 20

Transformed

About eight years into their marriage, two years after her double mastectomy, a year after her suicide attempt, Wally and Gracie decided to join a new church and plugged into a small groups program. One particular study changed their lives forever. Hungry for more in their relationship with Adonai, they chose to go all in with their heavenly Father. Adonai had strategically led Wally and Gracie to this point in their marriage to show them what He had next for them.

The study they were doing together helped Wally and Gracie find freedom from their past; Gracie found freedom from abandonment! Finally, after over fifty years, she was able to get healing and let the past go. Gracie made significant discoveries in her healing. She learned that she was wrong her entire life about her identity. Gracie had believed everything everyone said about her. She believed all the names people labeled her. Gracie always thought that she was set aside and that no one liked her. When there was a situation where someone picked teams, she was always the last one chosen; no one wanted her. She was too tiny and too quiet. Adonai revealed to her through the study that she was not set aside; she was set apart for a special purpose. That's why she didn't fit in; she wasn't supposed to.

Adonai had opened Gracie's eyes through this study. She could finally see the truth, Adonai's truth. She went headfirst, all in. Gracie prayed for Him to transform her; she allowed him to prune and refine her into what He created her to be. It was the same for the small group. She didn't even think of the ramifications of how much it would hurt to be pruned and refined. All she knew was that she wanted to be free from her past and who she had believed she was and to become what Adonai created her to be. She wasn't focused on the pain of pruning and refining. She knew that just like Adonai was with Moses bringing His people out of Egypt, He would be with her bringing her out of her personal Egypt. She had complete faith that He would help her bear the pain. She cried a lot, and it was painful. But as it turned out, it was bearable because He was with her every step. After that transformation, her prayers for pruning and refining became a regular occurrence for her to pray. As a result of her faith and the transformation to that point, she didn't beat herself up anymore when she would make mistakes. She learned to repent and move on. She no longer would park and pitch a tent and sit in the mud being pitiful. She learned how to admit her mistakes and ask for forgiveness and try to learn from the lesson and not make the same mistakes again.

Wally shared with Gracie how Adonai had healed many areas in his heart through the study as well. They were finally able to have peace in their love for each other (2 Timothy 1:7, Hebrews 11:6). There is no fear in love; perfect love casts out all fear (1 John 4:18). With the fears gone, Wally and Gracie could finally see how much they loved each other and enjoy their love.

Gracie's healing process was immediate and progressive. She felt like Adonai had healed her immediately from her abandonment issues and people pleasing, but other areas in her life were peeling back one layer at a time. Gracie let everything go. She learned that anything we focus on that isn't Adonai is an idol (Ezekiel 14:60, 18:30).

Suddenly she could see; Adonai had revealed the truth to her (Job 42:5–6). Gracie may have been abandoned, but she was never alone. Adonai showed her that He never left her (Hebrews 13:5, Genesis 28:15, Psalm 27:10). People left her, but He never did. Adonai showed her that He created her for Himself for a special purpose; He had set her apart. He created her to crave a love that only

He could fill. Gracie finally found real love, Adonai's love (Proverbs 8:17, 1 John 5:3).

By His grace, Gracie had turned from people pleaser to God pleaser. She no longer cared what others thought of her. Suddenly if someone didn't like her, Gracie was okay with it. When someone said unkind words to her, she learned to give grace and remind herself what Adonai says in His Word about her—chosen, holy, and dearly loved (Colossians 3:12, 1 Peter 2:9). That's not to say that people no longer said hurtful things to her. She isn't saying that she isn't affected by hurtful statements toward her. What she learned was to work hard alongside Adonai to become unoffendable. When hurtful things come her way, she has learned to give grace and give them to her heavenly Father. The Father blesses those who bless His people and curses those who curse them (Numbers 24:9). Gracie continues to work hard to trust Adonai to protect her.

Before Adonai changed her life, not only did she believe the mean things people had always said or called her, she called herself those names as well. That's why when she made a mistake, no one had to get on to her; she beat herself up with all the bad names she already heard and thought about herself. One of her small group leaders prayed off the ability to call herself negative names anymore. Prayer works, but it still took practice for her not to give in to the temptation to beat herself up verbally. The enemy is constantly attacking (1 Peter 5:8). When she slipped a couple of times and began to rebuke herself for a mistake, she was immediately convicted in her spirit and repented (Luke 15:10).

Gracie knew a girl from church that always said, "I know who I am in Christ" (John 1:12, 1 Corinthians 6:17, Genesis 1:27, Jeremiah 1:5, 1 Corinthians 12:27). It wasn't until she found freedom from the spirit of abandonment that she understood what her friend meant. Gracie discovered through her healing and freedom from her past who she was in Christ. Adonai taught her through His Word that He says who she is, not others. Adonai continued to open her eyes to other lies that she had believed. Gracie could suddenly see how much Wally loved her. It was like she was blinded to the truth all her life, and now she could see.

Gracie had other revelations through her new eyes. She was able to see that people were not her problem; she was her problem. Adonai showed her that her dad, mom, friends, and ex-husband were not her problem. Everyone has scars, issues, and problems that are personal to them. No one is to blame for people's problems; the enemy constantly seeks to devour; he gets the credit. We aren't fighting people. We are fighting the enemy (1 Peter 5:8).

It was in this revelation that she realized and could finally see that her mom loved her and had not spent Gracie's lifetime intentionally tormenting her and trying to prevent her from being happy. Gracie had spent the first fifty years of her life believing a lie from the enemy that her mom didn't love her, when in reality her mom loved her very much. The truth in the Bible says, "For we are not struggling against human beings, but against the rulers, authorities and cosmic powers governing this darkness, against the spiritual forces of evil in the heavenly realm" (Ephesians 6:12).

With her heart healed and eyes open, Gracie could now see those that she felt caused her pain throughout her life through different eyes. She could forgive them for their part, and she apologized for her part. The look on their eyes when she apologized were looks of shock. When she called her ex, he was speechless. The last thing he would have expected was an apology from Gracie. She couldn't control whether they believed her or not; she just knew that she had to apologize. The freedom and peace she experienced through this healing process were amazing.

CHAPTER 21

Empty-Nester Time!

With Caroline, their youngest, married, it was time for a new chapter in the life of Wally and Gracie post-healing, going all in with Adonai; they were excited to see what Adonai had next for them. They had a new lease on life, freedom from their past, eyes wide open, happy, in love, and ready to enjoy retirement together.

They had mapped out several trips they wanted to go on. Plans were made to redecorate their home. They were enjoying not having any daily responsibility for the kids; empty-nest life would be sweet. They felt very accomplished to have gotten two amazing kids through college without any permanent mistakes; that was something to celebrate! They were almost giddy at the thought of being alone and doing what they wanted. Finally, it was their time to enjoy life together and be happy, focusing on health and happiness in their newfound freedom from all their life's issues.

One Sunday morning, sitting in church holding hands with Wally, Gracie was trying to catch her breath from running around greeting people as she was settling into the service. Then all of a sudden, she noticed that feeling, that movement. She held her breath and waited. There it was again! She and Wally didn't get to sit and hold hands as often as she liked, but at church, she loved to snuggle up next to him and hold hands during the service. It was during the last few months that she had noticed something different during service holding hands. There was a twitching tremor that shot through his arm. When it first began, she didn't think much about it, but it seemed to become a regular occurrence. There were other signs of changes in him, but she ignored them and tried to pray the thoughts away. Today was different. It was like Adonai was saying, "Hey, pay attention." Gracie thought to herself, *Am I imagining things? Father, are you showing me something here? Please don't let it be what I'm imagining. Father, not now! You just healed us. Please don't let this be another battle to fight. Please don't test our faith already. Can't we enjoy our lives together for a while before the next battle?* All these thoughts kept running through her head at a rapid pace. Suddenly she had no idea what the pastor was saying or what was going on around her. All she could focus on were the thoughts running through her head. She knew what Adonai was saying to her. He was speaking clearly to her like a father speaks to their child; He had taught her to hear his voice. It was in this moment she wished she couldn't. Once you put your total faith in Him and give Him your whole heart and life, spend time in His Word getting to know Him and He sees that you are serious about your relationship with Him, He speaks to you clearly.

There was no use denying that she knew what He was doing and what He was saying. She was sad, but she trusted Him. In the middle of the service while all eyes were on the preacher, Gracie was praying, "Adonai, your will be done. If this is what is next for us, please give me what I need to fight this battle. Bless us, Father. We will continue to serve you. We will continue to trust you, no matter what comes." Gracie didn't need a doctor to diagnose. Adonai had already told her.

Today Adonai made her aware and told her to pay attention. The tremors in Wally's arm seemed more regular today; like every 30 seconds or so. She didn't say anything to Wally. Today, Adonai opened her eyes to start noticing his mannerisms. He is walking differently. He is sliding his feet and holding his arms in to his sides. His beautiful handwriting was getting noticeably smaller. His voice was getting quieter. What happened to his deep sexy voice? When did that disappear? Almost overnight it seemed everything had changed in Wally. In reality, they were told that once you are diagnosed with Parkinson's that you have had it for at least ten years or more. Suddenly so many things made sense. For years he fought extreme fatigue and sleep deprivation. When he did sleep, he wrestled wildly. They were told that those issues were related to his Parkinson's disease.

Before Gracie could get an appointment scheduled with a neurologist, he woke up one night with what they assumed was a reflux attack from the spicy dinner she had cooked. After not getting better two days later, she rushed him to the hospital where they later determined his gallbladder had ruptured. They were told that he should have died within an hour from that kind of damage. They nervously laughed and said it wasn't his time to go. It was then that his Parkinson's symptoms were magnified and could not be ignored. It took three months to get in to see the neurologist to confirm what they already knew but were then able to get on meds to help with symptoms. Wally and Gracie had been through a lot together and through many surgeries, but now they were in for the battle of their lives. This time though, they were fighting as dedicated children of Adonai, and together they would let Him fight this battle for them. They determined together that they would not listen to the enemies' lies and that they would trust Adonai every step.

Only a year after they had both found freedom from their past through healing from Adonai, they were on a new path, an unexpected path. It wasn't the one they had planned. While they were surprised, Adonai already had a plan mapped out. Now would come the real test. Were they going to trust Him with what was to come?

CHAPTER 22

The End of a Season of Life

The next five years were a blur. Gracie went into survival mode and stepped up into full-time caregiver mode. Health challenges they shared over the years, with this one being the most daunting, often would tear up most marriages. They heard through Parkinson's support group meetings of actual stories where the spouse left after diagnosis. Oddly, even though it was far from their plans for their future as empty nesters, his sickness brought them even closer than they already were. Nothing could stop their intense love for each other. It was a wake-up call that they didn't need to take each other and their time together for granted, a promise they made to each other when they married was to never take each other for granted and not to sweat the small stuff. Instead, they chose to stay focused on staying positive and to do as many things as they wanted to do together before they could no longer do them.

They had choices; be mad at Adonai or trust Him through this battle just as they had through all the others. It would be easier to take the easy way out, chose the wide path most traveled and blame Adonai and assume He abandoned them, allowing this disease to tear them apart. Wally and Gracie could feel Adonai's love in every step of their lives together; and they chose to take the road less traveled, the narrow path, and trust Adonai. Through the years, they had learned that trusting Adonai and clinging to Him through each life challenge got them through every step with amazing peace that is difficult to explain. They clung to Adonai, to His hope (Isaiah 43:1–3). They prayed together and decided that they would trust Him through this one too. Being mad at Adonai is counterproductive. When we are angry at Adonai, fear moves in and consumes us, causing countless problems. Trusting Adonai gives peace and hope. They clung to his promises. One of their favorites is John 16:33, "I have said these things to you, that in me you may have peace. In the world you will have tribulation. But take heart; I have overcome the world."

Gracie and Wally had unshakable faith by this point. Together they had survived so much, and each situation brought them closer to Adonai and closer to each other. They knew that no matter the outcome, Adonai would bless them and take care of them both.

Since the diagnosis five years prior, time had flown. They crammed as much fun into those five years as possible until Wally's body couldn't go anymore. Then one day, Gracie sat holding Wally's hand from his hospice bed in their den, tears slowly streaming down her face as their last days together were coming to an end. She listened to him talk about how much he loved her and how he didn't want to leave her or abandon her even though he was ready to be with Jesus. Gracie gazed at him with amazement as he had just recited the twenty-third Psalm by memory with such heartfelt emotion. It made them both emotional at hearing Adonai's encouraging words at such a time. For the past year, Gracie had read Psalm 91 to Wally every night. Even doing that one thing together each night brought them hope and joy even though their days together were quickly disappearing. They were reminiscing about the happiest years of their lives together; they laughed through tears as they remembered the fun and funny times and the not-so-fun times. He thanked her for letting him be himself, and she thanked him for loving her with all her baggage and insecurities. In doing so, they changed so much and allowed Adonai to transform them into who He created them to be. Even though they had lots of challenges in their marriage, to them, all their memories were good because they were able to do life together.

As she listened to him talk, she heard him say he didn't want to abandon her. When he said the one word that had haunted her throughout her entire life, she suddenly realized it didn't have the same hold on her that it used to. It was then that it struck Gracie that she was going to be okay. She thought back to how far she had come. The first important man in her life that she adored had abandoned her, and it rocked her world and affected all of her relationships. The second most important man in her life was about to abandon her in a sense too. This time, Gracie was going to be okay. In an attempt to calm Wally's fears, she said, "It's okay, babe, you can let go now. Adonai is going to take care of me. I will be just fine."

He looked up at her with a look as if she had just broken his heart. She gently said, "What is it?"

With sadness in his eyes, he said, "You used to always say that you couldn't live without me. We used to always say that we wanted Adonai to take us together. You don't love me anymore? You're not going to miss me?"

Gracie's heart just melted with love and renewed adoration for him at the sweet sincere innocence of his question. She responded, "Baby, no one could love you more than I do, and I'm going to miss you terribly. Before Adonai healed my heart, I had put all my trust in you for so many years. Even though I have always loved Adonai, my trust was more in you than it was in Him. It was unrealistic and unfair to you for me to do that; it put a lot of undue pressure on you. Adonai has taught me how to put all my hope and trust in Him, and in doing so, He has given me complete and amazing peace. Once He healed my heart and soul, I was able to love you in a healthy way."

As he searched her eyes in that moment, trying to process what she was saying, suddenly Adonai helped him see what she was saying; it clicked. Immediately he felt that same peace; he knew then that his baby was going to be okay. He could rest in peace now. With that peaceful thought, he drifted off to sleep again.

Adonai had brought her so far. He had healed her heart and shown her that her identity is in Him, not people. Gracie had gone from complete unhealthy dependence on Wally with a fear and extreme obsession for him to never leave her, praying that they would die together, then to do a 180 after Adonai healed her; she was no longer that person. Due to all the things Adonai had taught her and done in her, she knew that He would take care of her when Wally was gone. All those years they spent fearing the loss of either of them, Adonai had brought them so far and healed their hearts and souls. This happened because they invited Him into their marriage, their hearts, and life; and they allowed Him to change them.

Gracie spent her life wondering why people kept abandoning her and leaving her alone; why didn't people love her? Adonai showed her that people may have abandoned her, but she was never alone; He was always with her. Days later, when Wally peacefully passed away holding her hand, Gracie had amazing peace, not fear. She rested in Adonai's arms knowing that Wally was at peace with Jesus, and she could trust her heavenly Father's promises. She would never have to fear abandonment again. People may leave us, but our Heavenly Father is always with us. "I will be with you always, yes, even until the end of the age" (Matthew 28:20).

One of her favorite scriptures she clings to every day: Joshua 1:9.

> Have I not commanded you? Be strong and courageous. Do not be frightened, and do not be dismayed, for Adonai your God is with you wherever you go.

Days after Wally's death and celebration of life with friends and family, Gracie sat out on the patio one morning with her Bible in her lap and coffee in hand, listening to the birds chirping and the wind blowing, the chimes making a beautiful tune. Gracie looked up toward heaven praying and thanking Adonai for all of His blessings and for healing Wally and taking him safely home with Him. She assured Adonai that her life is in His hands, she is all His, and that she is ready for whatever comes next in the story of her life that He has planned for her. She prayed that Adonai would use her story to help inspire others to overcome their fears and find true peace, His Shalom peace.

APPENDIX A

Life Lessons

- We are never alone (Joshua 1:9).
- God always has a purpose in the pain.
- Whether it's His plan or someone else's, He will use it for His good (Romans 8:28).
- When we make mistakes, God can still use our mistakes for His purpose.
- Don't give up.
- Recognize and repent.
- He will forgive you and get you back on track.
- Get in His Word.
- Read the whole Bible, Genesis to Revelations.
- In the Word equals in relationship with Him!
- Not in the Word equals not in relationship with Him.
- We must have a firsthand relationship with God.
- We won't recognize the counterfeit if we don't know the original.
- Stay in the Word.

APPENDIX B

When Gracie read the story of Joseph, it sounded similar to her life in many ways. See if you see yourself in this story. The story of Joseph is found in Genesis beginning in chapter 37 and goes through chapter 50.

The parallels in Joseph and Gracie's stories:

- They both had dreams.
- Their dreams got squashed.
- The Lord moved them away from their problems.
- God taught them many lessons.
- He refined them.
- Pruned them.
- Tested them by fires.
- Lessons in the wilderness.
- They were both "chained" in their problems.
- They were imprisoned in their problems.
- He raised them both from their problems.
- He used their problems for His purpose.
- They both sought the Lord for help.
- He taught them both how to put their hope in Him.

- They both thought they were ready to go again before God was done pruning them.
- They both allowed God to work in them.
- He blessed them both and used them in mighty ways.

APPENDIX C

Transformation

See how God changed her and let Him change you.

Gracie had reached a level of heart healthiness that she could finally function as a much different person. Thanks to God and Wally, her self-confidence and self-esteem were restored. Gracie was blessed with boldness and courage after going through all of God's pruning and refining. The process was arduous and did not feel good at the time, but it sure felt great once she got on the other side of the lessons; she was a different person. Anyone who knew her before she gave her heart totally to God would not know the new Gracie; she is a different person. If someone didn't like her, it didn't crush her anymore.

Our identity is in Christ alone, not who or what others say we are. There is a season and a time for everything. Nothing is permanent. It's okay. Don't be afraid when a season ends. He has something even better waiting for you. She came to realize that God puts people in our lives for a reason and for a season.

He showed her several things about relationships:

- Sometimes He ends a relationship because He wants you out of it.
    - If you won't leave, He will pull you out painfully.

> - When friends she cared about walked out of her life, she was okay. Her hope was in the Lord, not people.

- It's impossible to see His plan if we are focused on what others think of us. We must focus on Him.
  - He will always show you right on time, His time.
- When God ends a relationship for us, either the relationship is toxic and He is removing us from it, or the season for that relationship is coming to a natural end.
- Trust Him.
  - Some seasons last longer than others, but they all come to an end.
  - Whether it be a friendship or marriage ending or a life ending, trust Him.
- He has a special plan for you, and it includes His Shalom peace if you trust Him to take care of you.

Since the diagnosis five years before, Gracie and Wally grieved together. After Wally's passing, Gracie was no stranger to the process. Gracie told Wally that she had no idea what she would be like after he left, but Gracie knew she would be okay because her hope was in God to take care of her. God gave her immeasurable peace. He gave her hope (Isaiah 43:1–3).

She recognized that she had never been alone; He was always with her in her wilderness. Gracie was no longer in fear of abandonment. She found complete peace. If God would do this for her, He would do it for anyone who turned to Him for help.

APPENDIX D

How to Find Peace

1. Enemies may gloat over you falling, but He is your light (Micah 7:8).
2. Know that God doesn't change (Malachi 3:6)
3. He will never leave you nor forsake you (Hebrews 13:5).
4. He is with you wherever you go (Genesis 28:15).
5. He works all things for His good (Romans 8:28).
6. Be strong and courageous. Don't be afraid; He is with you (Joshua 1:9).
7. Don't be anxious (Philippians 4:6–7).
8. He goes before you (Deuteronomy 31:8).
9. You don't have to be afraid or discouraged (Deuteronomy 31:8).
10. Even though others leave you, He will not leave you (Psalm 27:10).
11. He keeps looking for you (Mark 5:32).
12. Don't be afraid; keep trusting Him (Mark 5:36).
13. He is your stronghold in times of trouble (Psalm 9:9–10).
14. We are not alone (John 16:32).
15. Keep your life free of the love of anything but Him (Hebrews 13:5).
16. He sees you. He knows you. He's waiting for you to call out to Him (Mark 6:48).

Suggested steps to follow:

1.   Pray.
2.   Choose to give your heart to Jesus the Messiah.
3.   Seek Him. Seek a close relationship with Him.
4.   Read His Word from Genesis to Revelations, the whole Bible.
5.   Read it every day.
6.   The more time you spend with Him, the more He will show you.
7.   You will find Shalom peace.
8.   Pray for more of Him. He will give you all you want.
9.   Don't listen to the world; listen only to Him. His Word will tell you everything you need to know.
10. He loves you, and He says who you are.
11. Study His Word to find out what He says.

APPENDIX E

How to Pray

Your Father knows what you need before you ask him.

You, therefore, pray like this:

Our Father in heaven! May your Name be kept holy.

May your Kingdom come, your will be done on earth as in heaven.

Give us the food we need today.

Forgive us what we have done wrong, as we too have forgiven those who have wronged us.

And do not lead us into hard testing, but keep us safe from the Evil One.

For kingship, power and glory are yours forever. Amen. (Matthew 6:8–13)

APPENDIX F

$$Salvation\ Prayer$$

He's waiting. He's listening. Keep it simple. Pray something like this:

Dear Lord Jesus,

I know that I am a sinner, and I ask for Your forgiveness. I believe You sent Your Son to die for my sins and He rose from the dead. I repent and turn from my sins and invite You to come into my heart and life. I want to trust and follow You as my Lord and Savior. Amen.

> For I am not ashamed of the Good News, since it is God's powerful means of bringing salvation to everyone who keeps on trusting, to the Jew especially, but equally to the Gentile. (Romans 1:16)

> For he says, "At the acceptable time I heard you; in the day of salvation I helped you." (2 Corinthians 6:2)

> Pain handled in God's way produces a turning from sin to God which leads to salvation, and there is nothing to regret in that! But pain han-

dled in the world's way produces only death. (2 Corinthians 7:10)

That if you acknowledge publicly with your mouth that Yeshua is Lord and trust in your heart that God raised him from the dead, you will be delivered.

For with the heart one goes on trusting and thus continues toward righteousness, while with the mouth one keeps on making public acknowledgement and thus continues toward deliverance.

For the passage quoted says that everyone who rests his trust on him will not be humiliated.

That means that there is no difference between Jew and Gentile—Adonai is the same for everyone, rich toward everyone who calls on him, since everyone who calls on the name of Adonai will be delivered. (Romans 10:9–13)

APPENDIX G

Suicidal Thoughts?

If you are having suicidal thoughts, don't isolate! Isolation is the enemies' playground.

> Whoever isolates himself seeks his own desire; he breaks out against all sound judgment. (Proverbs 18:1)

Reach out to loved ones. Call the suicide helpline, 800.273.8255. Call out to God. Both are 24/7. The difference, God created you. He knows you. He can meet you where you are and give you what you need. If you need someone to talk to on the phone, God may actually use someone on the helpline to help you. There's no shame in calling them.

- God has a purpose for your life (Jeremiah 29:11, Proverbs 3:5–6, Ecclesiastes 3).
- Your days are numbered; He decides when we get to be in eternity with Him (Psalm 139).
- He always has His eye on you (Psalm 32:8).
- You are His own special treasure (Deuteronomy 7:6).

When the righteous cry for help, the Lord hears and delivers them out of all their troubles. The Lord is near to the brokenhearted and saves the crushed in spirit. Many are the afflictions of the righteous, but the Lord delivers him out of them all. He keeps all his bones; not one of them is broken. (Psalm 34:17–20)

APPENDIX H

Info about Abandonment

In our culture, it would be very hard to find anyone who has not been affected by pain in some form. Whether human or animal, no one is exempt from experiencing abandonment in their life. It's a part of life. When we understand that concept, we can better manage our reaction to it.

Abandonment can come in many forms, through a divorce, through death, through disagreements, misunderstandings, miscommunication, through illness, just to name a few. Abandonment can be permanent or temporary. All of us can experience this type of loss any time throughout our lives from various areas of our life.

What are some signs that show you are not handling the abandonment well and need help?

- You are giving too much of yourself.
- You are overly eager to please others.
- You are laser focused on being liked and accepted.
- You get paranoid that no one likes you or loves you.
- There is jealousy in your relationships.
- You experience separation anxiety.
- You are easily offended.
- You are very sensitive to feeling left out, overlooked, or set aside.

- You are jealous of others' relationships.
- You have trouble trusting others.
- You are feeling insecure about your relationships.
- You sabotage your relationships.
- You have a need to control others.
- You may have a need to be controlled by others to feel wanted.

How are we to manage our response to abandonment in a healthy way? How do we keep it from wrecking our lives? Who do we look to for help in effectively dealing with the loss? Is it possible to be happy after abandonment? The answer, God. God provides us hope, healing, and happiness. I pray my personal story on this subject and how I found hope, healing, and happiness encourage you on your path to healing.

> May Adonai bless you and keep you.
> May Adonai make his face shine upon you
and show you his favor.
> May Adonai lift his face toward you and
give you his peace. (Numbers 6:24–26)

ABOUT THE AUTHOR

Grace was inspired to write this book to share her true story on abandonment and how it affected all her relationships for many years until a switch flipped and changed her way of thinking, and viewing herself and others. Grace discovered in her process of healing, that abandonment does not discriminate, it affects everyone at some point in their life and usually many times throughout someone's life. She feels inspired by God to share her stories with others to help them find the same healing and peace that she discovered. Healing is there for everyone, but you have to be intentional about searching for truth, and choosing not to allow abandonment to define you.

Grace is a widow, mother, and grandmother who stays busy studying God's Word, reading, writing, and blogging. Through a series of many life lessons, as a result of some good and some not-so-good decisions, her testimony allows her to empathize and relate with women in many similar life experiences. Grace loves to share what God has taught her through her life and through her studies, and finds herself in a season where she is able to do just that. She believes that God has called her to encourage others and introduce them to "hope" in this dark world. Grace shares how to find healing in any circumstance so that everyone can experience lasting mental health and happiness. You can find more of her shares, and her shop, at: www.ChosenCrowned.one

Abandoned but NOT alone is the first book in a trilogy.